# K/R

# K/R

**Projects/Writings/Buildings**

**Introduction by John Keenen**
**Essays by Terence Riley**

**Photo Essay by Tim Davis**

**Ten Thousand One**

For LKK and MJR

Distributed throughout the world by
D.A.P./Distributed Art Publishers, Inc.
155 Sixth Avenue, Second Floor
New York, NY 10013
www.artbook.com

Design: Omnivore
Edited by Ann ffolliott and John Keenen

ISBN 978-1-933045-64-1
First edition
Printed and bound in Germany

"More Than Seeing" (pages 10–13) was originally published in a slightly different
form as "Sensuality," in *Perspectives* (Hamburg: Hoffman und Campe Verlag,
2004), revised 2007.

"The Architects' Room" (pages 130–133) was originally published in a slightly
different form in *Fabrications* (New York: Museum of Modern Art, 1998),
revised 2007.

"Light Construction" (pages 134–153) was originally published in a slightly different
form in *Light Construction* (New York: Museum of Modern Art, 1995), revised 2007.

Cover photograph by Tim Davis
Frontispiece: Ken Hayden, Detail of Court-Houses (see page 115)

Copyright credits for certain illustrations are cited in the Photo and Drawing Credits,
page 158.

www.tenthousandone.com

# Contents

1

2 3

4

5 6

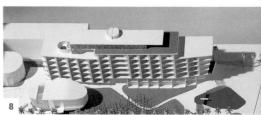

7 8

WE'RE
TALKING
JUNGLE

9

K/R

10 11

12 13

Buster Cooey
Electric
Page (213) 717-5122

# Introduction
## John Keenen

In the mid-1980s, the prospects for launching a new architectural practice in New York City were bleak. With tastes oscillating between bland commercialism and hokey historicism, worthwhile commissions were hard to come by and young firms struggled to survive. Competing against each other for projects that inevitably went to larger, corporate firms, they were often relegated to paper architecture, competitions, academia, and interior design. This phenomenon was well represented by the image of the "street-fighter," as described by Kenneth Frampton in his seminal essay "New York Narcosis," in *New York Architecture 1970-1990*. Street-fighters were known to be fierce by necessity: motivated, resourceful, and determined to leave their mark on the architectural land-scape, despite—and perhaps because of—the odds.

In operation since 1984, the studio of Keenen/Riley—now known simply as K/R—was founded in those street-fighting days as a means of reconciling our energy and curiosity with our desire to design, and ultimately, to build. Since our modest beginnings, we have witnessed the demise of post-modernism, endured economic market fluctuations (from Reagonomics to Irrational Exuberance), and watched our enterprise grow, shrink, and expand anew. All the while we have continually sought to explore pertinent issues of contemporary design, architecture, and urbanism, thus compiling a body of work as represented in this book.

Each of the projects contained within is different from the next, due in part to variations in program, client, and budget. What unites them is a process that questions and challenges accepted truths (both out of intellectual curiosity and restlessness), in hopes of gaining insights that might lead not just to theories, but to built form. As proclaimed by Roithamer, the anti-Architecture protagonist in Thomas Bernhard's novel *Correction*: "the word B U I L D is the most beautiful in the language…"

While building—reshaping the environment in a meaningful way—has always been a motivating force, collaboration has been our method. While perhaps not the most streamlined way to run a practice, it has proven to be a personally satisfying and most rewarding way of working.

Collaboration has expanded our thoughts, challenged our assumptions, inspired our visions, forged close bonds, taught us new ways of seeing and working, opened up fields, and shown us the value of our ideas as much as we may have sometimes questioned them. Ultimately, it has given us great joy in our work.

Collaborators have included friends, colleagues, artists, contractors, and, of course, clients—whose participation and encouragement have led to some of our most valued efforts. They have also included past and present employees of the firm, all of whom deserve our heartfelt thanks for their time, energy, and contributions (see page 156).

As we embrace our middle age, we feel fortunate to be part of a profession that values spontaneity and innovation as well as longevity and wisdom. We look forward to building upon our knowledge and the relationships that have sustained us these past years.

## Notes (pages 6-7)

1. Joel Sternfeld, *Ken Robson's Christmas Tree*, January 2001. Photograph. Looking south along the High Line, the only lights burning in the building on the right are in K/R's studio.

2. Terry Riley building a house of cards, 1989. This photograph accompanied a 1990 interview in *Prinz Magazine*, Bochum, Germany, about K/R's involvement in the Ruhrgebiet project in West Germany, the first time the firm was involved in an academic project abroad at the urban scale.

3. K/R's entry to the Cathedral of St. John the Divine Bio-Shelter competition, New York City, 1992. This invited competition—one in a long line of architectural competitions sponsored by the Cathedral during its history—called for the completion of the south transept using the program of a "bio-shelter" as developed by René Dubos.

4. Visitor Center, Khao-I-Dong Refugee Camp, Aranyaprathet, Thailand, 1980. Designed by John Keenen during a sabbatical between the first and second years of architecture school, this bamboo building—operated by the International Rescue Committee—sits just beyond the gate of the Khao-I-Dong Refugee Center, located on the Thai-Cambodian border. The camp has sheltered more than 50,000 Khmer refugees. The classical Khmer temple form inspired the double-pedimented design.

5. K/R T-shirt (orange/white), 1997. Modeled by Manuel Rodriguez. Beginning in 1997, K/R issued occasional T-shirts for staff, who chose the colors.

6. Keenen building a house of cards, 1989. This photograph accompanied a 1990 interview in *Prinz Magazine*, Bochum, Germany, about K/R's involvement in the Ruhrgebiet project in northwestern Germany.

7. Paul Nelson, *Maison Suspendu* (project), 1936-38. From *The Filter of Reason: The Work of Paul Nelson*, edited by Terence Riley and Joseph Abram, Rizzoli/cba, 1990. Published for an exhibition at the Ross Architectural Gallery, Buell Hall, Columbia University, Spring 1990, Riley's first curated architectural exhibition.

8. Aerial view of hotel and landscape, Miami Beach, FL, 2000. This project was designed as an oceanfront annex to an existing art deco hotel as part of an invited competition. It incorporates an extensive integrated landscape design.

9. Beauty, a K/R studio mascot from 1984 to 1987, in a still image from Bureau's "Rock the Vote" video for MTV, 1992. K/R shared studio space on West 14th Street with this graphic design firm during the 1990s.

10. Interior, new Dacra offices, Miami, FL, 2006. The program of this project was to create office space that functions both as art gallery and offices for this international development company. The client, Craig Robins, displays his extensive collection here on a rotating basis, thereby incorporating art into the workplace.

11. K/R T-shirt (green/black, sleeveless), 2001.

12. Yvon Lambert Gallery, West Chelsea, New York City, 2003. This New York branch of a Paris-based gallery epitomizes the white-box approach to gallery design: devoid of details, a neutral environment in which to exhibit contemporary art.

13. The Ruhrgebiet Model City, Bottrop, Germany: Master Plan. International Sommerakademie fur Architektur, Herne, Germany, 1989. John Keenen and Terence Riley, group leaders. Sponsored by IBA (International Building Exhibition Emsher Park), this summer academy focused on the development in the Ruhr industrial region of western Germany.

14. Riley's thesis project for his Master of Science in Architecture and Urban Planning at the Columbia University Graduate School of Architecture, Planning, and Preservation, 1982: Whitney Museum addition, perspective. His architectural interests were already focused on museums and projects in the public realm.

15. Interior courtyard, Court-Houses, Miami, Fl, completed 2005 (see page 115). Designed by K/R and John Bennett. Video by Matthew Weinstein, 2006. The north-facing courtyard wall was designed to serve as a projection screen for videos.

16. Andrew Bush, *Buster Cooey, Electric*, 1997. Photograph, 24" x 42". By a friend and frequent collaborator, from his series of photographs of business cards.

17. Tony Smith, *Olsen House* (site plan), 1951. Colored pencil on paper, $18 \frac{3}{4}$" x $23 \frac{7}{8}$". Keenen was co-curator, with Robert Storr, of the architecture section of the 1998 retrospective on Tony Smith at the Museum of Modern Art, New York. He later renovated this seminal house by Smith, with its elaborate site plan, from 1999 to 2004 (see page 92).

18. Pat Hearn Gallery (left) and Morris Healy Gallery (right), 1991. Gallerists began to move to West Chelsea in the early 1990s, as two of the first galleries—designed by K/R—open in a renovated taxi garage, on changing West 22nd Street. K/R opens a studio in West Chelsea in 1997.

19. Dogface, a K/R studio mascot from 1984 to 1987. Still image from Bureau's "Rock the Vote" video for MTV, 1992.

20. Searing House Addition, Montauk, NY, completed 1998. Designed for a friend, the distinguished architectural historian Helen Searing, this project was greatly enriched by the client's extensive knowledge of architecture and its history.

21. Aviary, Dominican Republic, 1998. Small Bird Cage (cage within a cage; see page 29). This was one of the more unusual K/R projects in that the birds were really the clients. K/R consulted with Don Bruning, an ornithologist with the Bronx Zoo/Wildlife Conservation Park, to gain an understanding of how the birds live.

22. Interior, Playboy International offices, Miami Beach, FL, 2000. The wall covered in varying tones of blue commercial-grade carpet defines a conference room within a large, open, unfinished space (see page 100).

23. Aviary #2, Mexico, 2001. K/R's second aviary, like the first in the Dominican Republic, was based on environmental and ornithological principals (see page 84).

24. Thomas Ruff, *d.p.b. 02*, 1999. Chromogenic color photograph, $51 \frac{3}{16}$" x $6' \frac{3}{4}$". From the *l.m.v.d.r* project (1999-2000), commissioned on the occasion of the 2001 *Mies in Berlin* exhibition at Museum of Modern Art, co-curated by Riley.

25. K/R T-shirt (grey/pink), 2003.

26. Bruno Jakob, *2 Architects Walking in an Invisible White Room*, 1991. Invisible drawing/water on paper. An artist who works with air, water, and energy, Bruno Jakob based this drawing on Keenen and Riley. It was a gift from artist.

27. Study Model, Land House, Pine Plains, NY, 1991. This unbuilt project has always seemed to form part of a trilogy of house designs: Mill House (see page 19), Land House, and Field House (see page 55).

28. Interior, New York City, 1998. Like many young New York firms, K/R learned much about materials, detailing, and tectonics while designing interiors, still a strong interest.

29. K/R T-shirt (burgundy/blue), 2000.

30. Detail, Light Monitor, Rowell Residence, New York City, 1998. The light monitor captures light from the larger loft to illuminate an internal room.

31. K/R T-shirt (light blue/white), 1997.

# More Than Seeing
## Terence Riley

Photography and architecture are allies. But a purely visual understanding of buildings comes at the expense of many other means of perceiving architecture's pleasures.

When photography was invented in the early nineteenth century, its first subjects were architectural—for obvious reasons. Due to its technical limitations, early photography needed a subject that was washed in daylight and that remained perfectly still.

Through photography, images of place-bound buildings have been disseminated throughout the earth. We are, to a certain extent, so influenced by this relationship that we have become overly reliant on visual skills while forgoing the use of other senses.

As a result of, or in reaction to, this acquired way of thinking about architecture, some of my most memorable architectural experiences have occurred in spaces that are difficult if not impossible to photograph. Unable to reduce the experience to a snapshot, a slide to be filed in a mental collection of architectural images, different faculties kick in to record, comprehend, and calibrate the experience.

### 01

A few years ago, I visited the Pulitzer Foundation in St. Louis, where Richard Serra's sculpture "Joe," one in his series of "Torqued Spirals" of two-inch thick steel ribbons, was installed in an exterior courtyard. It is around dusk as I enter the thirteen-and-a-half-foot high, 125-ton steel nautilus. Compressed in this seamless channel, the rusting surfaces suddenly seem less like heavy metal and more like sheets of lush velvet. As the passage narrows I feel the day's heat radiating from the steel, making me realize once again how thick and heavy Serra's ever-bending surfaces are.

### 02

When I was a university student I lived in Rome for a year and nearly every day I would visit the Pantheon. One of my most distinct memories of the space is auditory. Despite its platonic beauty, there is a slight nervousness to the space and its sounds. The circular plan and vaulted dome provide no horizon, no static frame for the eye to rest upon while hard materials—marble revetment and pavers below and volcanic tufa above—conspire with curving surfaces to create acoustical anarchy. For whatever reasons, low frequency sounds—deep voices, for example—disappear into space while higher-register sounds permeate. A soft but constant shooshing sound—like brooms on the pavement or raincoats brushing against one another—fills the air. It sounds as if someone is whispering in my ear but no one is near me. Twenty years later, I am in Bilbao in Frank Gehry's vast vaulted gallery and I recognize the same sounds.

**03**

Several summers ago, I had the chance to visit Peter Zumthor's so-called spa in the town of Vals in a mountainous region of Switzerland. I say "so-called" because the term "spa," with all its connotations of indolence, does not seem to capture what is really going on there. To me the experience was, indeed, therapeutic, but for the mind as well as for the body.

Attached to a pre-existing hotel and built into a steep slope, Zumthor's project is easier to feel than to visualize. To get to the spa, I descend through the hotel into the earth: the perfect sort of path for suggesting a transformative experience, a Parsifal scenario for activating the senses. After leaving my clothes and other articles of daily life—cell phone, wallet, keys—behind, I find myself in a damp, somewhat dark environment punctuated by streams of light from above.

The main spaces are a series of interlocking open areas with shallow steps leading into pools of water bounded by massive walls with equally massive piers that rise up out of the pools and provide central support. The walls and the piers are made of the same greenish marble, cut into long flat slabs and stacked in the manner of ancient Roman brickwork. The arrangement of the three pools further references classical themes: a frigidarium, a tepidarium, and a caldarium contain, as did the Roman baths, cold, lukewarm, and hot water, respectively. Becoming intensely aware of how well the body functions as a measure of experience, it suddenly seems silly that everyone is wearing a bathing suit.

Yet another pool is filled with not only hot water but also mountain flowers so that the chamber is filled with a sweet smell. Another chamber is only accessible through a portal below the surface of the water. Once inside the enclosed space, there is no soft material to absorb sounds and even the slightest whisper finds harmonic amplification from the stone and water. Positioned in a corner, I make what would otherwise be a barely audible humming sound, yet it reverberates, amazingly, like a powerful musical instrument.

**04**

Another Pantheon story. Some fellow students and I buy about 20 balloons and release them in the Pantheon. As they rise through the space, we realize how large in scale the coffers in the ceiling actually are and how that fact changes our perception of the space. We release all of the balloons in the center of the structure, but we notice they are moving differently as they ascend, revealing all sorts of micro-climatic conditions. On one side of the Pantheon, where the sun is streaming in, the air is warmer and the balloons rise faster and straighter. On the cooler side the balloons rise more slowly and disperse more broadly until they reach a certain height where a stream of rising air grabs them and whips them through the oculus.

**05**

The Gallery of the Horyuji Treasures—a relatively new museum in Tokyo—is dedicated to displaying magnificent artifacts from an ancient temple in Nara. Mainly of wood, paper, and textile, these works are very fragile and the light in the galleries is very subdued. I am in the main gallery. A bronze wall serves as a screen and backdrop to the individually illuminated artifacts. Oddly, it seems to me, two columns puncture the relatively small space. I ask the architect, Yoshio Taniguchi, about his intentions.

He explains that all the famous temples of Japan were wooden structures. The most important of them were also the largest and, because wood was not very reliable for spanning great lengths, they usually had two columns, one on either side of the statue of Buddha in the center. And the bronze wall? Temple bells are all made of bronze, and the architect hoped that the bronze wall as well as the two columns might subliminally suggest the objects' original setting.

## 06

Another story about Rome and proportion: Ten years after my student days, I am in Rome on vacation. The cardinals are meeting in the Sistine Chapel to elect a new pope. All of Rome goes to St. Peter's Square to see who it will be. Soon after the white smoke appears, the cardinals come out on the side balconies of the Basilica. I knew that Michelangelo had over-scaled all the elements of the façade to match the scale of the vast piazza, but I had never realized how much. The cardinals need to stand on ladders to see and be seen over the balustrades. Once they are assembled, I squint and it looks as if the balconies contain flower boxes filled with red geraniums.

## 07

After September 11, 2001, I was continuously asked why I thought that the public liked the "Twin Towers" while architects have been very critical of them. It occurs to me that part of the public fascination might have been related to their "twin-ness." Due to their uncanny replication of each other, twins not only fascinate, but they have the strange ability to make "non-twins" feel incomplete.

## 08

I consider the Sagrestia Nuova—the Medici Chapel—in Florence to be a seminal work of architecture but, at the same time, I have no idea what its exterior looks like. Even so, I don't think of it as a room; it seems like a small city. When I enter the room, time seems to slow slightly, like a change in tempo in a musical piece. Everything seems slightly more somber. Is this because it is a tomb? Or does Michelangelo's space actually slow you down, creating what Octavio Paz called a "vertigo of delay"? Or both?

Ultimately, I realize that part of this sensation is caused by the fact that there is really no place for me in the chapel. Even the open space is densely inhabited by the invisible lines and planes of an exquisite proportional system that I feel as much as understand. I get a similar feeling from the Casa del Fascio in Como by Giuseppe Terragni.

I sense my body being measured by the space even as I measure the space by walking through it. Blank "windows" frame the portrait statues. They are tall and wide enough for the sculpture of Lorenzo de Medici but too shallow for a real body. It is an uneasy feeling: If I leaned as far forward as the marble figure appears to be, would I fall?

It might be my imagination but does the space seem "tighter" than others do? Do the compositional elements fit together more precisely than they do elsewhere? Somehow it seems there are no gaps, less air, more stillness.

I try to explain this feeling to Colin Rowe, the illustrious architectural historian and theoretician. He nods and says that walking through the Sagrestia Nuova is like walking through the ceiling of the Sistine Chapel.

## 09

Until 1986, when it was rebuilt, very few people knew Mies van der Rohe's Barcelona Pavilion except from black and white photographs. A friend of mine showed me his diary entry from the day he visited it: "Walking through the pavilion, I become aware of what space is for the first time, the way a fish might come to understand water, if it could."

For me, the real shock is the color. I had mistakenly come to think of the Pavilion, like an ancient Greek temple, as a composition in whites and grays. How different it is to see the Pavilion's polychromatic reality. Training my eyes to focus on the surfaces of the materials, I also become intensely aware of the incredible series of reflections in the water, glass, chrome, polished marble and onyx. In layer upon layer of retinal pleasure, I find the reflection of myself in the marble, an otherwise unseen guard in the glass, and more. Could this really have been Mies' intention? Where is the austere functionalist that the post-modernists had railed against?

## 10

I wasn't there, but I was told about an architect who lingered inside Le Corbusier's chapel at Ronchamps after closing time. Brazenly, he lit a cigar and filled the space with as much smoke as possible so that he could see the light coming through the colored glass of the curving west wall more vividly.

## 11

A final story about Rome: I am in St. Peter's Square. A crowd has gathered near Bernini's Scala Regia, the monumental work of architectural theater that serves as the Vatican's diplomatic stage. I go to see what's happening. The Pope, all in white and gold, is coming down the stairs. The Queen of England is walking towards him wearing what looks like a traditional bridal dress except for the fact that it is as black as coal. She is wearing diamond rings and bracelets over black gloves, a diamond necklace and a diamond crown over a cascading black veil that covers her face. At the same moment, she curtsies a little and he bows a little and they walk up Bernini's stairs together, without touching. It is nine o'clock in the morning.

## 12

I am at the Glass House with Philip Johnson and Peter Eisenman, and we are sitting by the pool looking back at the house. Peter's then young son is in the guesthouse looking for his bathing suit. Unable to find it, he walks naked across the yard and into the Glass House in the unselfconscious manner that only a child can affect. The house suddenly seems more transparent, more stage-like and—most of all—more playful.

KR, a.k.a. Craig Costello.
Brooklyn wall, 2000.

Proj

ects

# 01/Mill House

LAMBERTVILLE, NJ, 1988

… Invoking the topos of the casino—according to [John] Keenen "a building type largely forgotten in the 20th century"—in response to the challenge of creating a game room and screened-in porch/terrace out of one of the small existing structures scattered around the grounds of a modest weekend house, K/R converted this first opportunity to build a free-standing structure into a primer for a personal architectural syntax.…

With its multiple entrances, the casino functions, at least symbolically, as a passage between two levels: the yard of the house on the crest of the slope and a leveled-off terrain around an outdoor swimming pool closer to the stream. Recognizing the potential of this hermetic fieldstone box—a mere twenty-eight by thirty-five feet in plan—the architects set themselves the challenge of confronting their long-standing interests in a highly articulated lightweight constructive vocabulary of modern industrial materials with the inert mass of an historical artifact, a sort of primitive degree zero of building. But from the first, this unassuming *objet trouvé* became an active partner in a lyrical dialogue of materials, structure, and space. Rather than an inviolate, historical relic preserved with some false sense of piety, the stone base became the support, both literally and figuratively, for a collage that emerged from the juxtaposition of heavy and light, closed and open, masonry and cage, crafted and tooled, rustic and refined. As Riley explains, "We worked and worked the collage until stone lost its privileged position of being preexistent."

K/R's additions were essentially two: a small but spatially complex volume to the side of the mill house for a new kitchen, toilet, and secondary entrance; and on its roof, a porch/belvedere of interlocking steel and mahogany frames. This porch, reached by a steel and wood-lattice gangway, provides an equivalent open volume to the found closed volume of the mill house. The two volumes are left as contrasting states of elementary enclosure; on each level services and circulation have been removed to the periphery to create an openwork modernist collage of lightweight planes and sliding spaces in counterpoint to the closed geometry of the masonry and screened volumes.…

Excerpted from "Tectonic Collage" by Barry Bergdoll, in *Perspecta 28, The Yale Architectural Journal*, MIT Press, 1997.

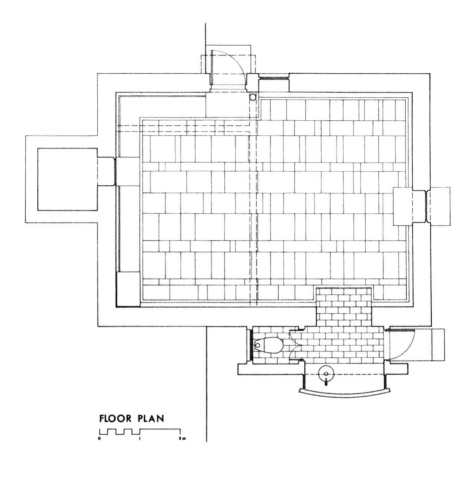

**FLOOR PLAN**

0   1   2m

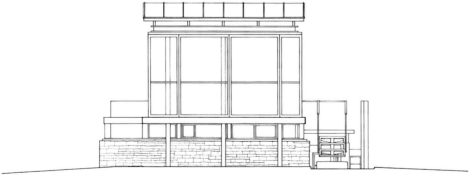

NORTH

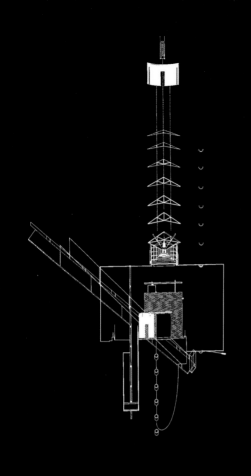

# 02/BoatHouse/ Footbridge

**NEW YORK CITY, 1987**

The BoatHouse is situated on a sliver of land between Manhattan's FDR Drive and the East River. It is composed of two main elements: a concrete block structure and a storage shed that is sheathed in corrugated steel over timber posts. Connecting these two elements is a curved wall of marine plywood. This wall extends up through the roof to hold a canopy over the viewing deck. Within the BoatHouse it supports the spiral stair and also screens the changing room and bathroom.

The front elevation carries a rolling door, which facilitates the movement of the twenty-meter shells. The height of the entrance is determined by the oars, which are stored vertically in racks opposite the stair. The shells are stored on racks attached to the timber posts. In this way, the structure that supports the exterior sheathing also supports the shells within. The shed is illuminated by means of a large skylight.

The construction of the shed mimics the structure of a racing shell—a frame with light-weight sheathing. This correspondence between the container and the object contained is further manifested in the form of the shed roof, which makes allusions to the upturned keel of a racing shell. The skylight makes further reference to this allusion.

The footbridge can be described as an asymmetrical bowstring truss, one quarter of which cantilevers over the water's edge providing a moment for viewing the city. The access ramps are integrated with the bridge's vertical supports. On one side this support is more massive, acting as an anchor. On the river side the vertical support is expressed as a screen wall that defines the BoatHouse court.

In the spirit of "Critical Regionalism," we have tried to integrate the use of universally produced materials (concrete block, corrugated steel) with elements that are more specifically inflected (curved wall, sloping roof line, and skylight). This contraposition of the universal and specific addresses the requirements for a relatively economical structure without sacrificing the possibility of a singular architectural event.

The racing shells provided us with more than a structural lesson. We have also tried to learn something from their other qualities: light weight, simple form, fragility, and functional elegance. These combined characteristics reveal an image of extreme purposefulness, Like a violin, it becomes impossible to separate the image from the use.

inset/**South elevation.**

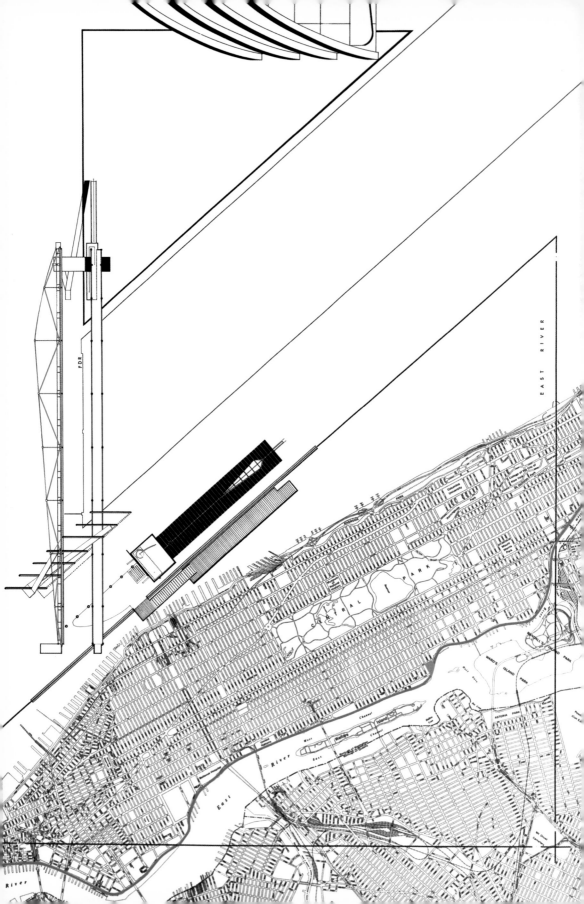

opposite page/**Site plan.**
below/**View from above.**
bottom/**Footbridge landing (looking east),
with boathouse beyond.**

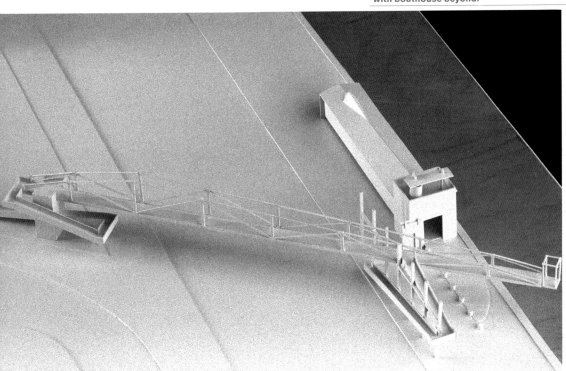

# 03/Aviary

**DOMINICAN REPUBLIC, 1998**
Built overlooking the Caribbean, this large aviary in the Dominican Republic offsets human and bird scales in elevated walkways and "invisible" mesh so that the two groups alternate in their changing roles as viewer and viewed. The construction is an unusually successful mix of local building methods—even the red stucco of the two L-shaped freestanding walls is a reference to the islands indigenous colors—and advanced steel structural forms that lessen its impact on the land. The deliberate crookedness of the tubular steel structural hoops mimics the trunks of nearby palm trees and, more ironically, the legs of the flamingos that live in the aviary. "Invisible" stainless steel mesh forms a diaphanous barrier between humans and birds. Perhaps the best testament to the aviary's success in integrating new and traditional construction is the fact that, of all the surrounding structures, it was the only one to survive Hurricane Georges virtually unscathed.

Excerpted from "Buildings for Living: Casa Di Uccelli/
Bird House" by Patrizia Malfatti, in *Arbitare*, February 2000.

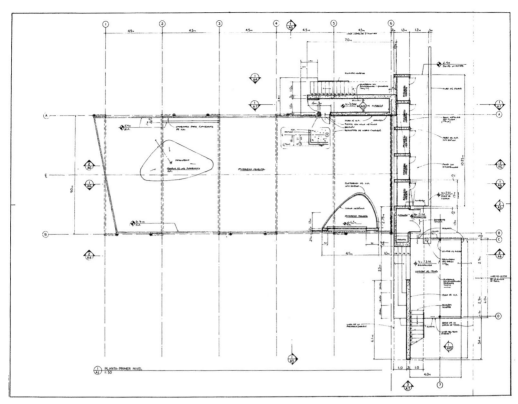

PLANTA-PRIMER NIVEL 1:50

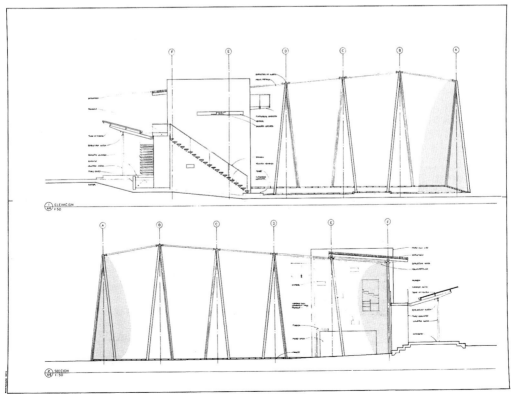

ELEVACIÓN 1:50

SECCIÓN 1:50

# 04/Townhouse

**NEW YORK CITY, 1999**

The divisiveness of the horizontal plane, repeating itself ad infinitum along Manhattan's vertical strata, did not deter K/R in the firm's efforts to unite the modestly-sized levels of an existing four-story building....

K/R designed the new garden façade as a curtain wall made of stucco, metal, and glass. From the outside, it reveals the spatial arrangement of the interior by expressing the floor slabs and vertical slots along with the variation in program along the different levels. From the inside, the wall has been carefully designed to mediate the flow of air, light, and views. Keenen improved an otherwise undistinguished backlot view by deftly combining clear, sandblasted, and prismatic glass panels. Clear sections were used at eye level and behind the frosted acrylic balustrade to create oblique garden views and guard privacy; sandblasted glass panels bring in additional light; and prismatic sections, composed of two pieces of clear glass laminated with an intermediate prism, refract light into the interior.

A new mahogany staircase, the physical link among levels, was located at the building's eastern edge. Between the garden and the street levels, the stair wraps around a new, cast-in-place concrete wall that anchors the steel structure above. On the entry level, the stair is separated from work areas by a screen fabricated of blued structural steel and mahogany slats....

Perhaps the most important built element that knits the interior together is the vertical screen between the work areas and the stairwell. According to Keenen, this construction subtly evokes a church's choir screen, which separates altar from choir but still allows for some transparency and view. This ecclesiastical reference is but one of several, coordinated ways that K/R reached for the sublime in their effort to render the everyday life of this foundation glorious.

Excerpted from "Golden Section" by Henry Urbach, in *Interior Design*, September 2000.

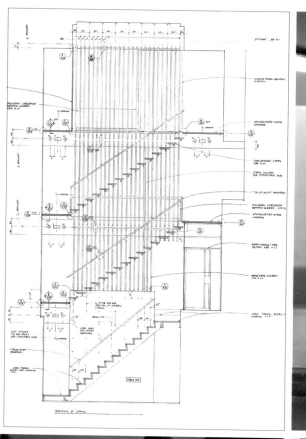

opposite page, top left/**Section through stair.**
opposite page, top right/**Reception.**
opposite page, bottom left/**Garden level.**
opposite page, bottom right/**Stair screen.**
below/**South façade.**

# 05/La Escuela

**LONG ISLAND CITY, NY, 2000**

The old warehouses, abandoned factories, and deserted streets of Long Island City, New York, made it a picture-perfect setting for a recent episode of *The Sopranos* that featured Tony crossing the East River for a tête-à-tête with a mob boss. The car pulls up, however, not at a shady loading dock or gritty storage facility but in front of a decidedly polished one-story structure hovering over an austere gravel yard....

When not making cameos on HBO, this structure is actually the new entrance to a three-story industrial building recently converted into work space for landscape designer Edwina von Gal....

The original entry sequence of von Gal's building was rather unwelcoming. Once inside the front door, she immediately had to ascend a flight of steps to the main level, which is actually the second story. To improve upon this off-putting sequence and gain a reception area in the process, K/R erected an elevated addition that cantilevers over the gravel front yard. Von Gal now ascends a painted steel exterior staircase to reach a lobby at the height of the main level. Although actually resting on a concrete support that protrudes from the original structure, the 900-square-foot addition looks like it's hovering off the ground, explains Keenen: "It appears light in contrast to the building's heavy masonry."

K/R set the addition five feet apart from the original building and connected the two with a hallway. The reveal highlights distinctions between old and new, as do differing materials and treatments. The addition is clad predominantly in panels of lightweight composite board made to look like cement, contrasting with the brick of the main building.

Excerpted from "KRQNS" by Sheila Kim, in *Interior Design*, November 2002.

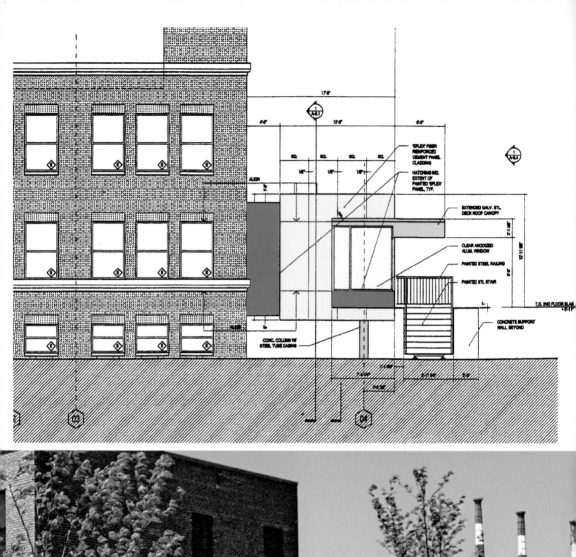

opposite page, top/**South elevation.**
opposite page, bottom/**South elevation.**
below/**Corner detail.**

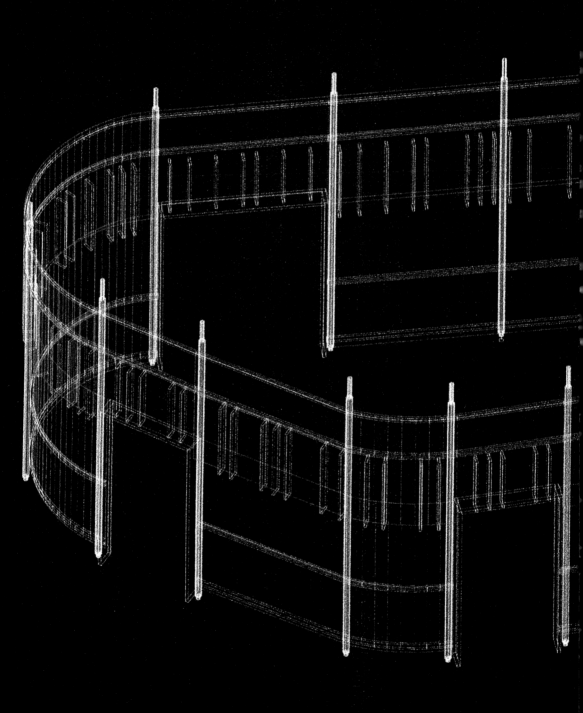

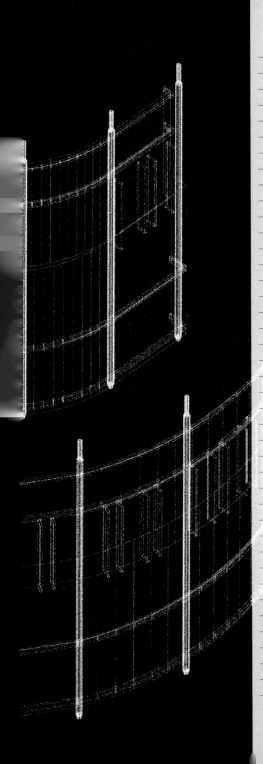

# 06/CTG Offices

**MIAMI BEACH, FL, 1998**

The Cisneros Television Group, based in Miami's South Beach, is a new company that creates broadcasting channels in Latin America and throughout the world. Its first office, designed by New York–based K/R, aims for what principal John Keenen terms "a refined rawness".... The 18,000-square-foot space retains much of its original concrete structure, exposed ductwork, and lofty expanse while also accepting new elements that give spatial order, programmatic definition, and more than a touch of tropical tang....

A limited palette of materials and articulate tectonic gestures unify the entire floor. The existing concrete structure was sandblasted, and concrete floors polished and exposed everywhere but the entrance and lounge/lunchroom, which were covered in coco matting and linoleum respectively. Aluminum, acrylic, and basswood are the other major materials. The extensive use of translucent acrylic provides a loose, permeable sense of spatial definition as light and silhouette play across its surface.

The four affiliate channel offices are organized around a space that Keenen calls the "belly," a rounded secondary lobby and passageway defined by a curving screen of acrylic panels mounted on an aluminum frame. The panels, held away from the floor to emphasize spatial continuity, give privacy while allowing light to pass; during the day, the belly is lit by natural light from the perimeter, while at night it glows with artificial light to animate the adjacent channel offices. K/R used two vertical layers of acrylic sheets and "stitched" them together with basswood fins that establish an intermediate scale and impart another, softer texture to the space. Where the belly opens to the channel offices, there are wood-lined portals without doors.

Excerpted from "The Raw and the Cooked" by Henry Urbach, in *Interior Design*, May 1998.

drawing/**Study of transparent wall system in "the belly."**

opposite page/**Channel entry.**
below/**Conference lounge.**
bottom/**Entry to conference lounge.**

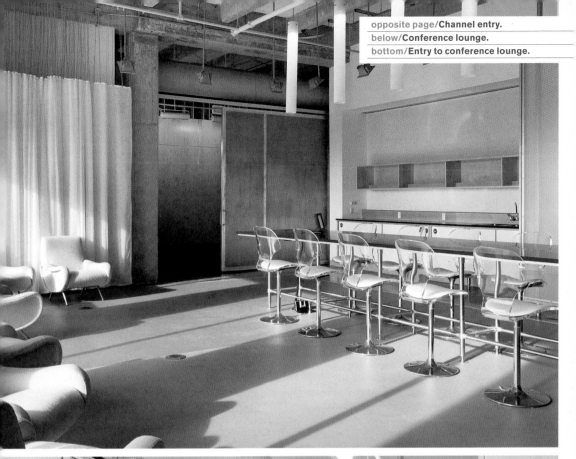

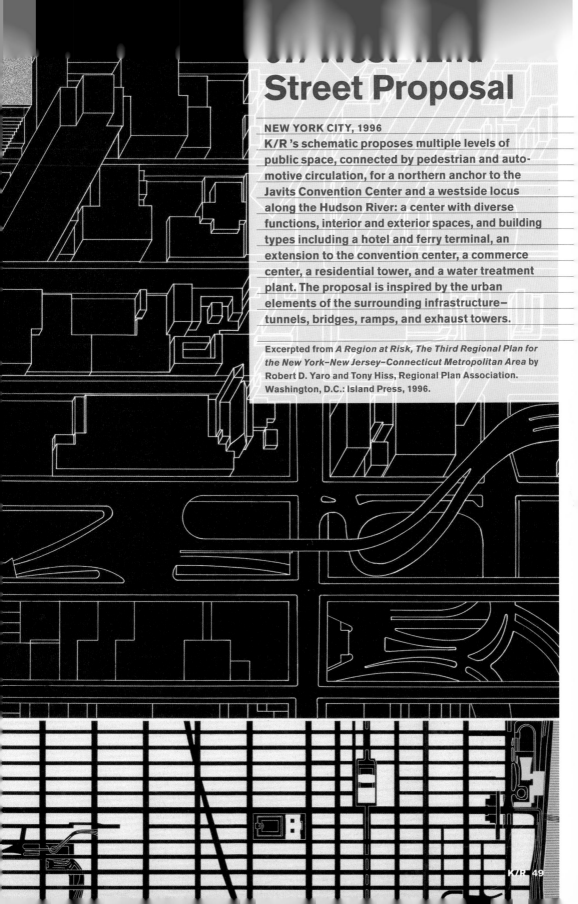

# Street Proposal

**NEW YORK CITY, 1996**
K/R 's schematic proposes multiple levels of
public space, connected by pedestrian and auto-
motive circulation, for a northern anchor to the
Javits Convention Center and a westside locus
along the Hudson River: a center with diverse
functions, interior and exterior spaces, and building
types including a hotel and ferry terminal, an
extension to the convention center, a commerce
center, a residential tower, and a water treatment
plant. The proposal is inspired by the urban
elements of the surrounding infrastructure—
tunnels, bridges, ramps, and exhaust towers.

Excerpted from *A Region at Risk, The Third Regional Plan for
the New York–New Jersey–Connecticut Metropolitan Area* by
Robert D. Yaro and Tony Hiss, Regional Plan Association.
Washington, D.C.: Island Press, 1996.

# 08/Tuttle Street

**MIAMI, FL, 2004**

Like Eadweard Muybridge's photographic studies of the body in motion, the concrete façade of this two-story gallery building is conceived as a progression of fragmented movements, which when viewed from a passing car appear animated. The board-formed poured-in-place concrete fins fronting the street radiate outward, responding to the curve of Tuttle Street, a semicircular street that forms the eastern entrance into the developing Design District in Miami.

A series of corner windows anchor the predominantly open ground floor and continue up to the second floor, where they act as reveals between consecutive panels of concrete. Woven stainless-steel mesh screens protect the expanses of glass on the southern façades, allowing for views out while veiling activities within the second floor during the day, depending on angle and light.

The interior has been designed with a flexible open plan and a strategically located central stair allowing for multiple possible tenant configurations and methods of build-out. The shell of the building has been engineered to the strict standards of South Florida hurricane code. The construction is scheduled to begin in 2007.

below/"Ascending Stairs" and "Looking Around with Basin in Hands" by Eadweard Muybridge.

opposite page, top/**Street façade.**
opposite page, bottom/**Site plan.**
below/**Entry.**

# 09/Field House

**WESTERN NEW JERSEY, 1997**

The design of this house is largely in response to the issues of privacy associated with building in an open field, a sixteen-acre corner site surrounded by farmland in western New Jersey. The house is situated in the farthest corner of a pasture and is seen as a low-lying, horizontal collection of buildings, not unlike the seemingly random arrangement of agrarian structures of neighboring farms.

The architects' initial strategy was to treat the design solution as a landscape problem. While the pasture at first appears completely flat, there are subtle variations in the ground plane. These variations were exploited and incorporated into the overall design. The buildings are cultivated into the site, capturing and framing major and minor views. What first appeared as a non-landscape was, in the end, the major organizing force behind the design.

The buildings are sited so as to turn their backs on the two roads at the opposite corner of the property. The two main buildings face onto a semi-enclosed yard, which in turn opens to capture oblique views of an adjoining field to the south. This siting also affords the main house an equally important view, looking west over neighboring fields and toward distant hills.

The main space of the house is the living room, which straddles the yard on one side and the west-facing terrace on the other. In addition, the first floor also holds the other main functions of the house: a dining room, kitchen, screened-in porch, and two bedrooms. The second floor contains a library that overlooks the inner yard and two additional bedrooms. The guesthouse (to be built as part of a second phase) will include a tool shed, guest suite, and pool cabana that will open onto a shaded poolside patio.

Excerpted from *The New American House 3: Innovations in Residential Design and Construction*, edited by James Grayson Truelove and Il Kim, New York: Whitney Library of Design, 2001.

Landscaping by Dan Kiley; decoration by Sills Huniford Associates.

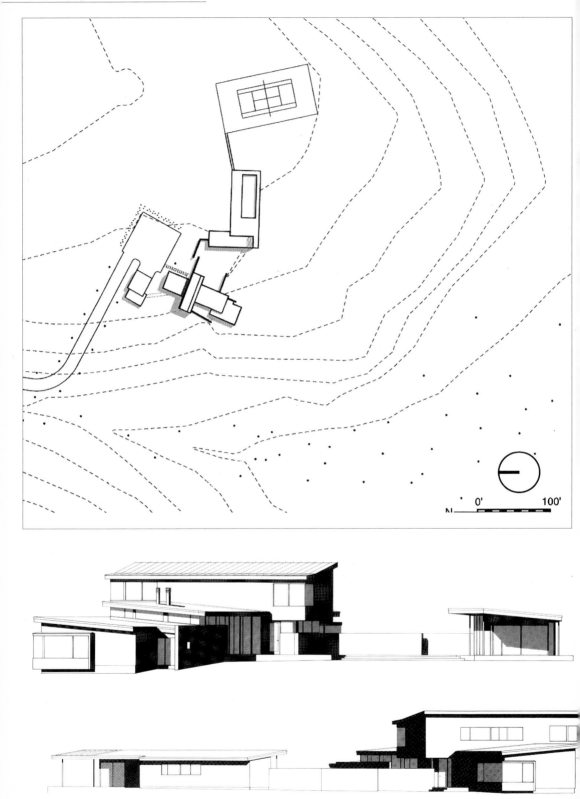

below/**On the west side, looking north toward terrace.**
bottom left/**Steps at courtyard.**
bottom right/**Detail, west façade.**

opposite page/**Screened-in porch.**
below/**Living room, looking west.**
bottom left/**Kitchen.**
bottom right/**Roof detail.**

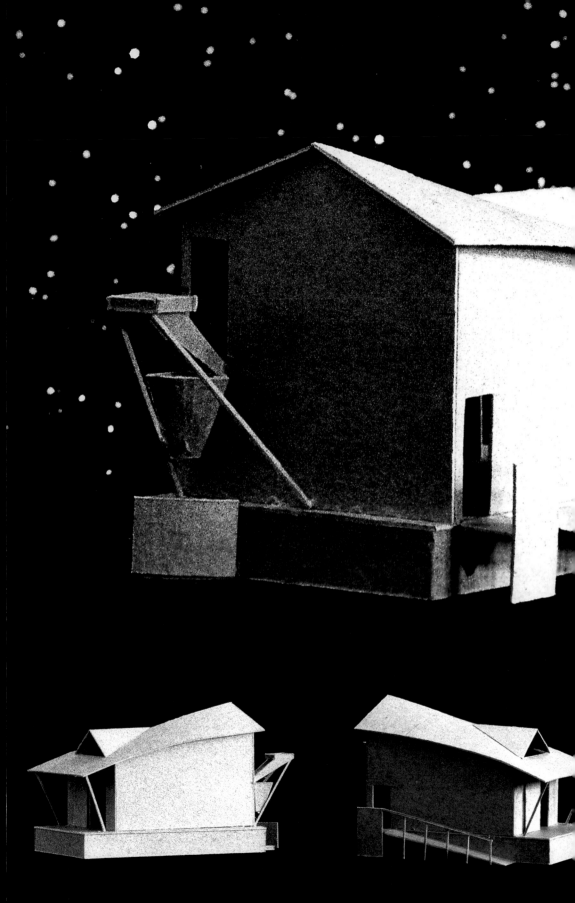

# 10/Sky Cabin

**NORTH HAVEN ISLAND, ME, 1985**

The cabin, or "camp," is meant to serve as an interim shelter for camping vacations and will be converted to a studio workspace once the summer house is constructed.

The primary purpose of the cabin is to provide shelter. All of the amenities are of an extremely basic nature: a wood-burning stove, hand-pumped water supply, propane gas cooking, a sleeping loft, and a "crows nest" for skywatching. There is a gravity shower beneath the crow's nest.

Except for the crow's nest, the cabin is all wood frame constructed on a base of granite, which is quarried on a neighboring island and is used throughout the area in a utilitarian manner. The stone base is elongated at one end to form a basin under the gravity shower. The wall sections are marine plywood with battens and clapboard on two-by-fours without insulation. The roof construction is standard two-by-six joists with multiple layers of thin plywood covered with asphalt shingles.

Around the turn of the century, North Haven supported a small year-round population of fisherman and sheep farmers. In addition there was a seasonal population of "rusticators." The term refers to off-islanders from various points on the eastern seaboard, many of them wealthy, who made an annual trip to North Haven. As opposed to the more opulent homes they might have had in Newport or other places, the rusticators built camps—more simple structures—on the island. Rather than a pleasurable vacation, rusticating was more of a retreat with an underlying moral premise.

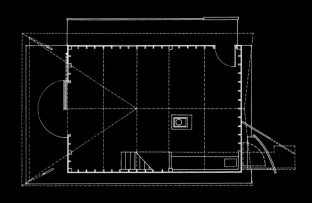

# 11/Exhibition Design

*Tony Smith: Architect Painter Sculptor*
Museum of Modern Art, New York, 1998
John Keenen, co-curator with Robert Storr and exhibition designer
of architect section

*The Un-Private House*
Museum of Modern Art, New York, 1999
Terence Riley, curator and exhibition designer

*Mies in Berlin*
Museum of Modern Art, New York, 2001
Terence Riley, co-curator with Barry Bergdoll and exhibition designer

*Poul Kjaerholm and Selected Artists*
Sean Kelly Gallery, New York, 2004
John Keenen, curator and exhibition designer

Philip Johnson Galleries, Design Collection
Museum of Modern Art, New York, 2002
Terence Riley, exhibition designer

*Glass + Glamour: Steuben's Modern Moment*
Museum of the City of New York, New York, 2003
John Keenen, exhibition designer

In glass, designers of all kinds have found an alchemic union of strong and fragile, organic and synthetic, volcanic and Neptunian, aqueous and mineral. In designing the Glass + Glamour exhibition for the Museum of the City of New York, John Keenen of K/R has made glass both subject and object. The intimate room-within-a-room that sheathes an existing 5,000-square-foot colonial revival gallery in faceted white walls suggests a bright, mineral underground. The gallery contains 200 pieces of mid-20th-century modernist glass by Steuben, while also containing visitors within the exaggerated prisms of a glass-like vessel. "I like the idea that the space is somehow analogous to the inside of a crystal object," says Keenen. By simultaneously mimicking and contracting the material on display, the architecture unexpectedly rescues itself from scrutiny. Opaque walls frame a transparent horizontal vitrine that belts the room and, lit from within, provides the sole source of illumination. Blue and purple inflections enlivening the white backdrop are underscored by a blue (and, happily for Keenen's tight budget, inexpensive) Astro-Turf carpet. Crunching under-foot, the carpet tends to slow visitors down, literally, while providing an earthy contrast to the ethereal designs. The tall display island that floats in the center of the room creates a path of circulation, and, by reflecting reflections, its mir-rored surfaces play on the metaphysical qualities of a material that trumps the eye, suggesting the endlessness of both space and imagination.

Excerpted from "The Glass Menagerie" by Shonquis Moreno, in *Frame*,
May/June 2004.

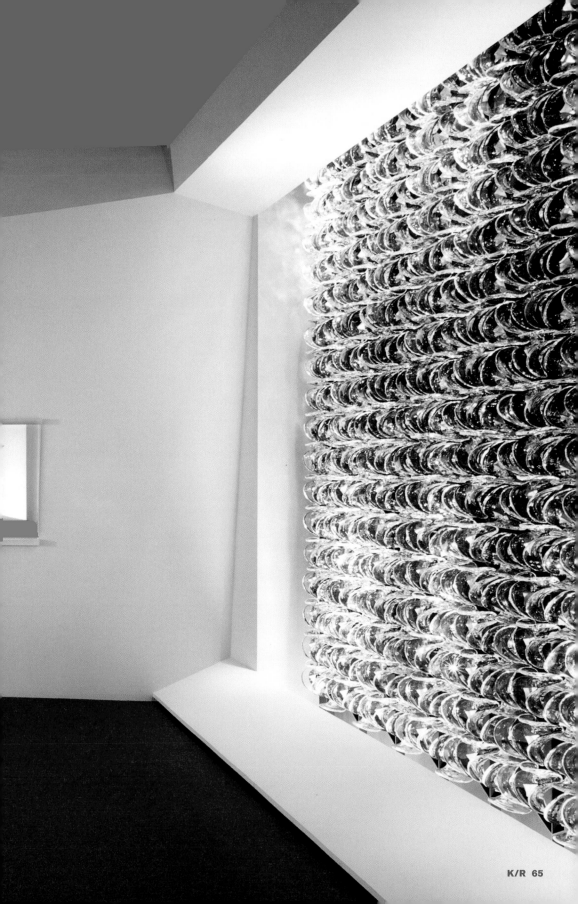

below/**Interactive display, "The Un-Private House."**
bottom/**"Light Construction."**
center/**"Glass + Glamour."**

below/**"Tony Smith,"** with Bennington
Structure in foreground.
center/**"Poul Kjaerholm,"** chair PK13,
**1974. Hanging sculpture by Liam Gillick.**
**Wall installation by John Lindell.**
bottom/**Philip Johnson Galleries, Museum**
**of Modern Art, New York.**

# 12/Flight

In his book, *Six Essays for the Millenium*, Italo Calvino predicts a new relationship in the technological world: the "heavy machines" of the 20th century will still exist, but they will obey the command of "weightless bits." In other words, the Machine Age will not be totally eclipsed by the Cyber-Age. Rather, the new century will be best represented by a hybrid of technologies working together to achieve greater efficiencies and potentialities.

The well-designed airplane of today has the potential to symbolize Calvino's vision of the future: part machine, part computer, the aircraft in the digital age sails thorough the skies supported by not only the laws of mechanics and aerodynamics but by a stream of electronic data as well. In this way, the space of the airplane becomes endless. The dual power of its engines and its computers merges cities, continents, and differing time zones, eliminating the boundaries of "here and now." In the same spirit, on-board activities become seamless. The interior of the aircraft is no longer a single-function space for transportation but has become a multi-task environment that can be an extension of land-based activities.

Like Constantine Brancusi's sculpture, *Bird in Flight*, or Frederick Kiesler's *Endless Theater* project, the airplane describes a path whose form is fluid and continuous, moving between fixed points. The form of the aircraft responds to both. An invisible axis, about which the form is laterally symmetrical, runs through the length of the airplane and reflects the vector of forward motion toward nature's own axis: the horizon, limitless and ever-receding. All other aspects of the aircraft's form are subordinate to this function. Maximized speed and minimized inefficiency depend on the optimal interpretation of the laws of aerodynamics.

K/R's design for a functional, flexible, and luxurious machine for living and working reflects both the clarity of these engineering principles as well as the poetry of movement that underlies the aircraft's conception. These design principles have been applied to a specific scenario: an airplane that can accommodate eight people, for three weeks, for a trip spanning three continents. The group comprises a mix of CEOs, business associates, and family members. This particular scenario requires that the airplane be designed to satisfy overlapping needs for working and living, reinforcing the need for flexible space.

The concept of Endless Space is formally expressed in large-scale elements, such as the contour of the interior section, and in small-scale elements, such as the shape of the seats. Weight and fire safety requirements have been used as an inspiration leading to material innovation.

Excerpted from "Endless Space" by Terence Riley, from an entry to a design competition sponsored by Boeing, 2000.

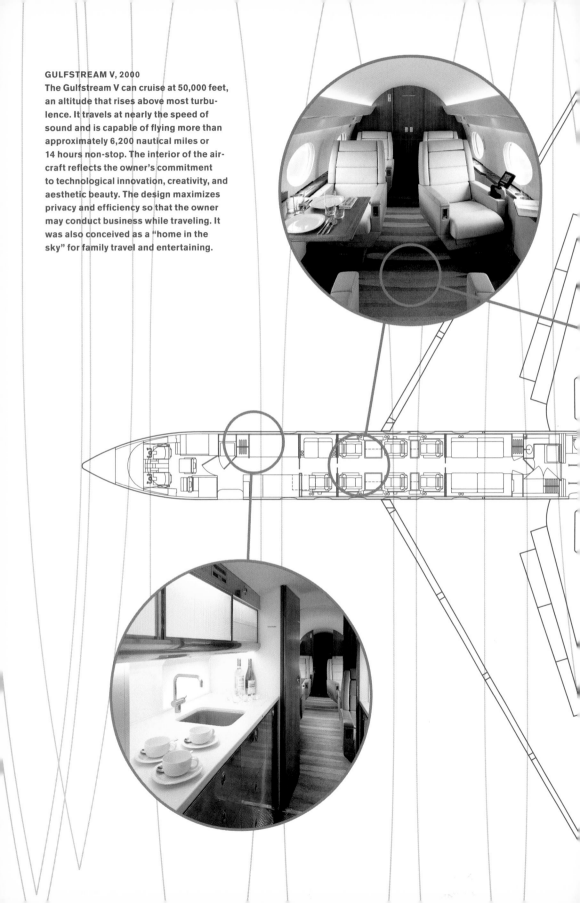

**GULFSTREAM V, 2000**
The Gulfstream V can cruise at 50,000 feet, an altitude that rises above most turbulence. It travels at nearly the speed of sound and is capable of flying more than approximately 6,200 nautical miles or 14 hours non-stop. The interior of the aircraft reflects the owner's commitment to technological innovation, creativity, and aesthetic beauty. The design maximizes privacy and efficiency so that the owner may conduct business while traveling. It was also conceived as a "home in the sky" for family travel and entertaining.

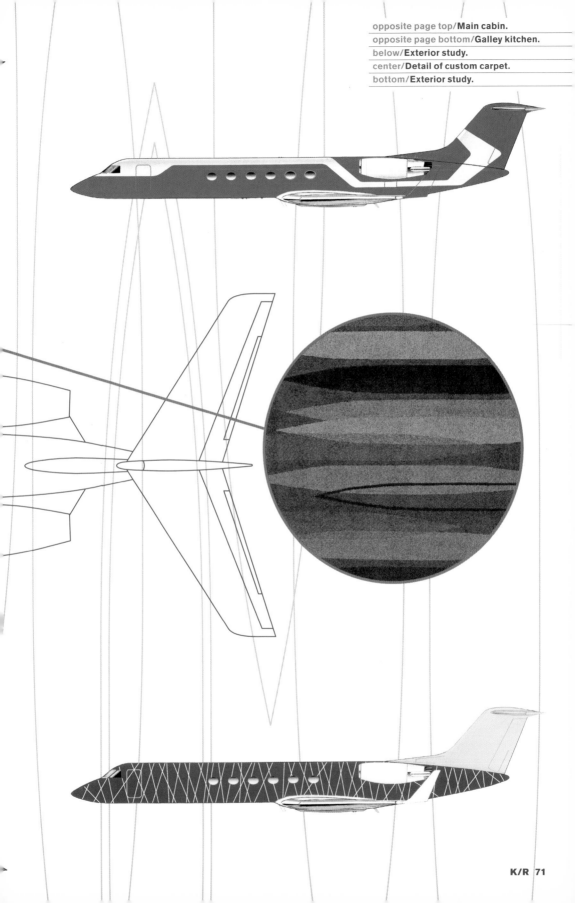

opposite page top/**Main cabin.**
opposite page bottom/**Galley kitchen.**
below/**Exterior study.**
center/**Detail of custom carpet.**
bottom/**Exterior study.**

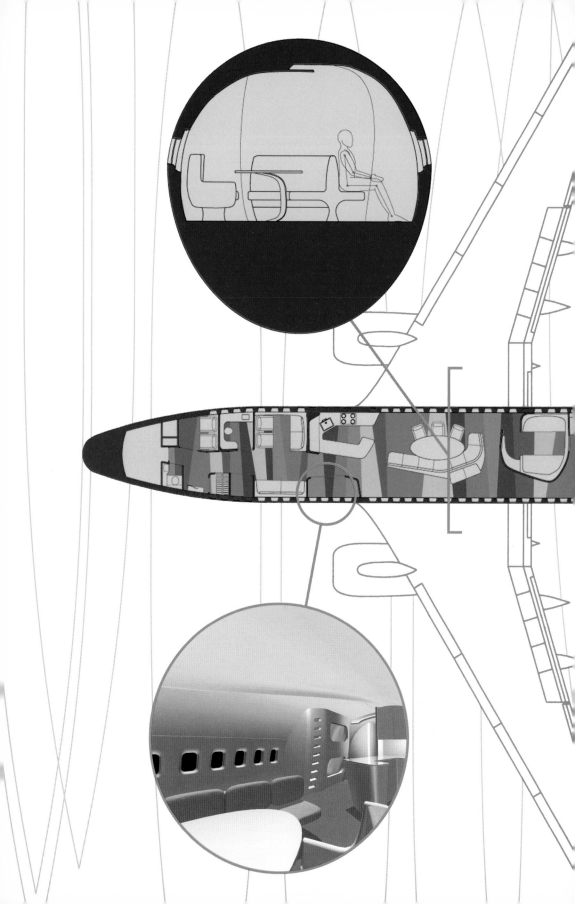

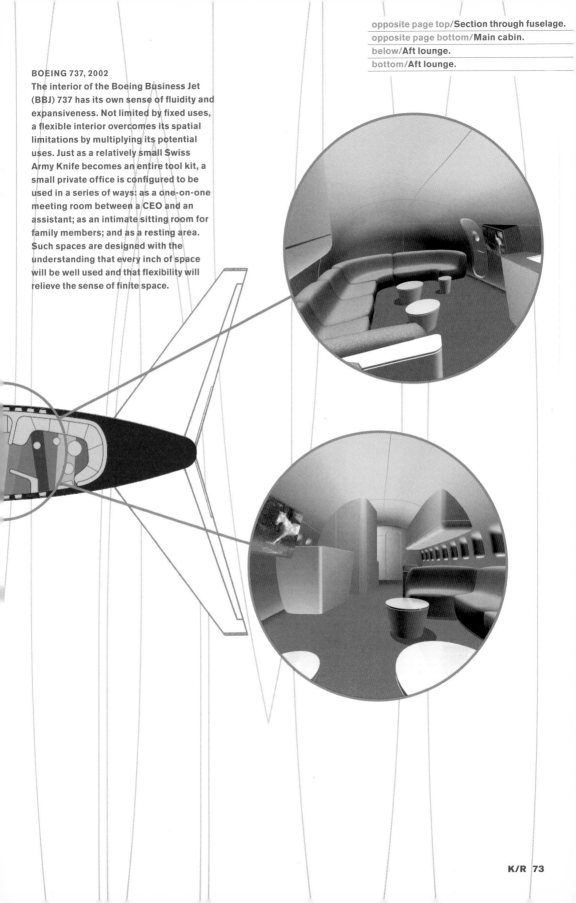

opposite page top/**Section through fuselage.**
opposite page bottom/**Main cabin.**
below/**Aft lounge.**
bottom/**Aft lounge.**

BOEING 737, 2002

The interior of the Boeing Business Jet (BBJ) 737 has its own sense of fluidity and expansiveness. Not limited by fixed uses, a flexible interior overcomes its spatial limitations by multiplying its potential uses. Just as a relatively small Swiss Army Knife becomes an entire tool kit, a small private office is configured to be used in a series of ways: as a one-on-one meeting room between a CEO and an assistant; as an intimate sitting room for family members; and as a resting area. Such spaces are designed with the understanding that every inch of space will be well used and that flexibility will relieve the sense of finite space.

# 13/Bronx School

**BRONX, NY, 1991**

The idea of community is critical to our proposal for a new school for Morrisania. In dealing with the complex program for making three schools, we chose to make one unified building to house all three. In doing this we saw the potential for a school that would function not just as a school, but also as a center that deals with social and cultural concerns of the community.

Standing on the edge of Clinton Avenue, the building takes on a linear form. This "bar" serves to mediate between the two worlds: the street world of the Bronx and the world of the school as created by the series of enclosed public spaces and courtyards found within the inner block.

The main entrance to the school is located on Clinton Avenue and is marked by a large cylinder that functions as the circulation core. From this entrance one moves to the individual schools and community-related services. To the left on the ground level are the day-care/toddler centers and health-care facilities. Above these spaces is located the elementary school. Above this is located the middle school (floors two and three) and the high school (floors four and five). Located at the back of the bar, creating an inner sanctuary for those using the school, are the larger and more public spaces: the day-care/toddler center, dining hall, gymnasium, and auditorium. These spaces are organized around three outdoor courtyards....

Both the ground level and the top floor, or "sky deck," hold the common spaces shared by all three schools. The ground level is articulated as a continuous base, which supports the floors of the bar above. The sky deck holds an outside gymnasium for the grammar school and a common library for all students.

Excerpted from *New Schools for New York: Plans and Precedents for Small Schools*. The Architectural League of New York, The Public Education Association, New York: Princeton Architectural Press, 1992.

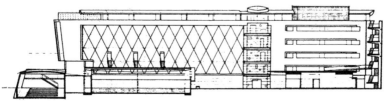

COURTYARD ELEVATION

TYPICAL FLOOR

ROOF LEVEL

# 14/Palm Island

MIAMI BEACH, FL, 2000

Technically speaking, this is a renovation. But if one considers the scope of the transformation of this Miami home on an island in Biscayne Bay, the term "alchemy" seems far more appropriate. John Keenen of the New York firm K/R has changed lead into gold, converting an anonymous, crumbling, 1950s modern house into a contemporary refuge of extraordinary intimacy, refinement, and character. The metamorphosis is dazzling....

.... To open up the landscaping possibilities on the wedge-shaped property, Keenen did what few architects and clients do in these "more is more" times: he made the house smaller. By excising a decrepit carport and various inelegant additions, the architect freed the front yard for use as a dramatic arrival sequence. He then called upon landscape designer Edwina von Gal, a frequent collaborator, to realize his grand vision of environmental chiaroscuro....

Inside the main gate, von Gal installed two large, low mounds—one planted in monkey grass, the other in selaginella —that lend the courtyard a quality of biomorphic abstraction. Beyond them she placed a bamboo grove that shields the front façade of the house and surrounds an outdoor sitting area. She covered the driveway in crushed black obsidian to enhance an atmosphere she describes as "mysterious and inward." She and Keenen added a moat along the front façade....

Keenen accentuated the open plan of the first floor of the house, which joins the living room and dining area in one spatial sweep, with large expanses of glass offering views of the bay. Presiding over this arena is a sculptural staircase made of free-floating terrazzo treads on a spine of tubular stainless steel. The second level became a single master suite comprising a bedroom, a dressing area, a den, and a bathroom contained in an oval enclosure clad in walnut veneer....

Keenen is primarily an architect—he's at work on a new master plan for the Miami Design District—but he relishes the roles of interior decorator and art adviser. Here, he paired lesser-known mid-century Italian and American design with art by Yayoi Kusama, Tony Smith, Yves Klein, and others. "It all really suits," Keenen says. "The whole process has been about creating an identity for a place that never really had one."

Excerpted from "Playing It Cool" by Mayer Rus, *House and Garden*, March 2002.

Landscaping by Edwina von Gal.

opposite page, clockwise from top left/
**Curved wall, master bedroom; pool,
with Biscayne Bay beyond; Master suite.**
below/**Spina de pesce staircase.**
following spread/**Garden room with moat.**

# 15/Aviary 2

**MEXICO, 2001**
Aviary 2, a light-weight construction made primarily of invisible stainless steel netting, is to be located along the mountainous Pacific coastline of Mexico, in the town of Careyes. Perched on the edge of a cliff, the design is an exercise in landscaping and structural engineering. Following a strict program dictated by basic ornithological principles, the intended residents are indigenous tropical birds of Mexico.

  A network of paths guide the spectator from an upper garden, down the slope, and ultimately through the aviary. Once inside, the viewer becomes an observing guest in a house of birds. From within, two distinct environments can be experienced: a densely planted jungle-scape, which rests on terra firma, and a cantilevered free-fly zone, which projects upward toward the sky, with views of the sea beyond.

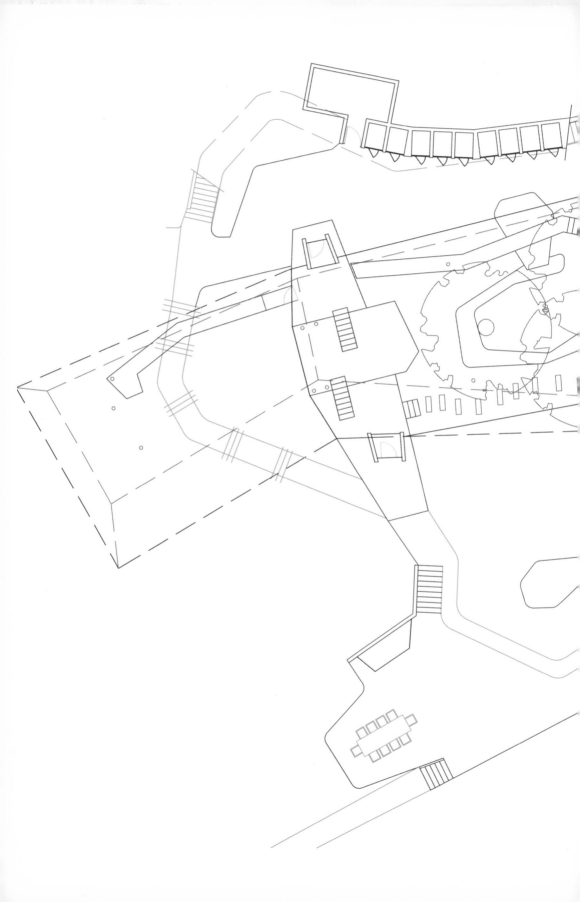

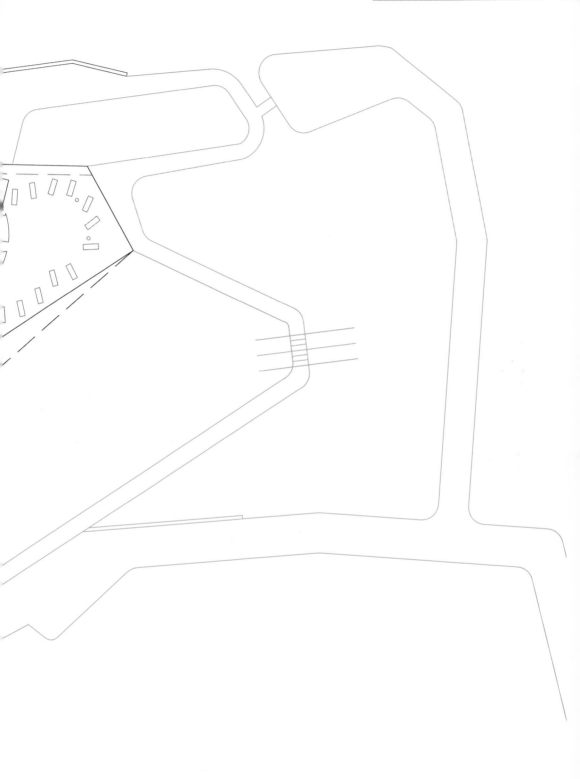

# 16/Palm Court Building

MIAMI, FL, 2004

Highway 195, a major east-west thoroughfare in Miami, connects the city with the barrier island known as Miami Beach and forms the southern boundary of Miami's Design District. From this elevated roadway, travelers will have excellent views of the future Palm Court Building.

Located on the corner of Palm Court and NE 39th Street, this 120,000-square-foot, twelve-story mixed-use building is the first in a series to be built, according to a Design District Master Plan developed in part by K/R.

The Palm Court Building is programmed for a variety of functions, including residential, commercial, and retail. The third floor—which formally acts as a "reveal," separating the base from the tower above—is reserved as public gallery space. It is reached by a designated two-story glass lobby, which anchors the southwest corner. The entry aligns with a newly created mid-block pedestrian mews, which connects NE 39th and NE 40th streets.

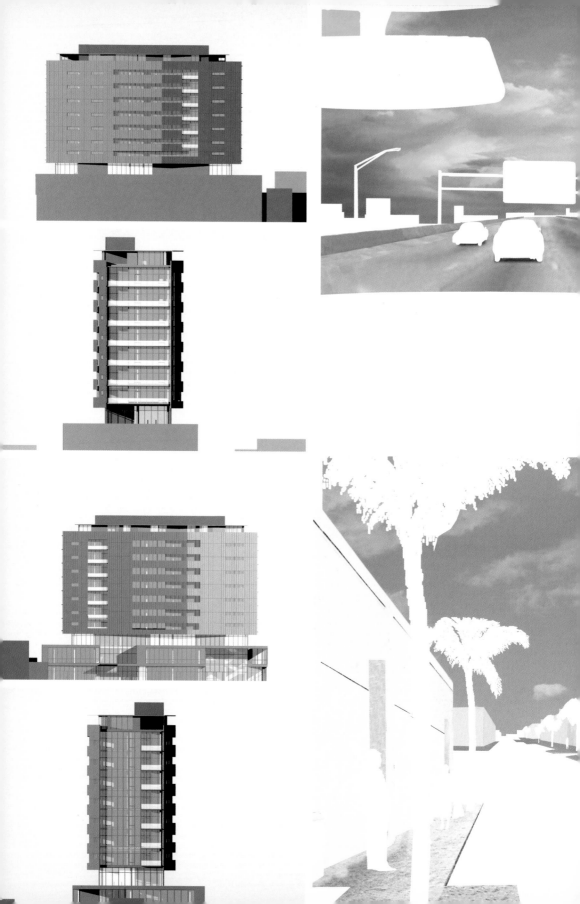

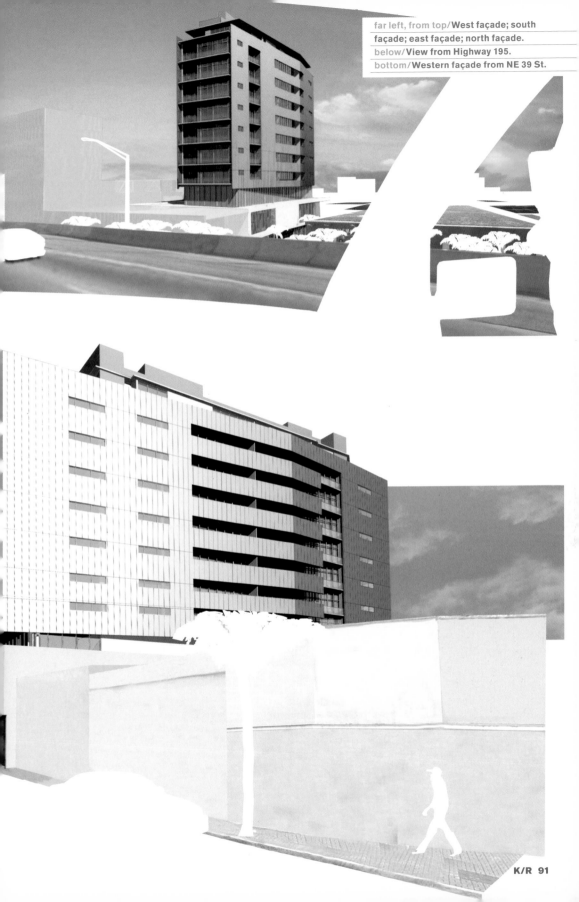

far left, from top/**West façade; south façade; east façade; north façade.**
below/**View from Highway 195.**
bottom/**Western façade from NE 39 St.**

# 17/Tony Smith's Olsen House Revisited

GUILFORD, CT, 1953

K/R's restoration/renovation, 2005

.... The essence of the design was Smith's skillful master plan.
Two primary elements define and organize the existing site and
the buildings that sit upon it: one was the existing topology,
and the other, a formally applied geometric patterning, superimposed by the designer. It was the layering of these two
organizing devices that gave the site plan an overall complexity, integrity, and visionary beauty.

Smith used the highest point on the property—a natural outcropping of stone—as the center of origin for the plotting of the
overlapping geometries from which the buildings are gener-
ated. Radiating outward from this point is a series of concentric
circles whose edges touch the rim of the cliff that marks the
limit of the site. Within the circumference of the outermost ring
(which has a radius of fifty-one feet), Smith inscribed a five-
pointed star oriented due north. Connecting the points of this
star, he then outlined a pentagram, which marked the dimensions and site location of the three building components: a
studio that housed the clients' art collection; the main living
quarters; and the guesthouse....

The concentric planning was further exploited by setting the
three structures at different elevations, suggesting an upward
spiral. The studio is on the lowest part of the site, the main house
takes up the middle ground, and the guesthouse is elevated on
rough-hewn timber *piloti*. The three are then connected by a
series of paths and covered ramps and are further joined on the
northern edge by an amorphic, if slightly awkward, pool that
wraps itself around the central rock outcropping. Each of these
buildings could stand alone on its own merit. As elsewhere,
traces of Smith's various architectural influences can be noted,
yet they are enriched and transformed by the relationship Smith
created between the buildings and their sites, and thus become
representative of Smith's particular vision.

Excerpted from essay by John Keenen, in *Tony Smith: Architect, Painter,
Sculptor* by Robert Storr, with essays by John Keenen and Joan Pachner.
New York: The Museum of Modern Art, 1998.

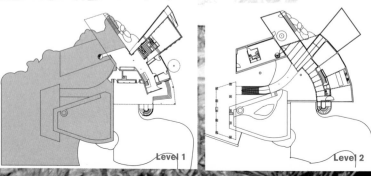

Level 1          Level 2          Level 3

K/R 93

46

47

48

49

K/R 99

# 18/Playboy International

PHOTO ESSAY BY TIM DAVIS

MIAMI BEACH, FL, 2000

"We were trying to break away from Playboy's connotations," says New York–based architect John Keenen about the new Playboy TV International offices in South Beach. (The company, a joint venture of Playboy Entertainment and Cisneros Television Group, develops TV networks around the world.) Keenen, who also designed Cisneros Group's Miami offices, says he was given free rein to interpret the South Beach program.

Visitors walking down the hall toward the sixth-floor Playboy office see an antiseptic-looking reception area through a glass wall. "For better or for worse, we wanted the approach to this very shiny white area to jolt you past any preconceived notions about the company," says Keenen. Inside the office, white is everywhere—from the gridded ceiling of frosted luminous Plexiglas panels to the glossy Formica custom furnishings. The whiteness gains even more wattage from the Florida sunlight that floods the floor.

A David Hockney painting of a swimming pool, which hangs above a couch in the reception area, is the first element to interrupt the austere flow. Five shades of blue standard-grade commercial carpeting break up the individual offices. The carpeting appears again on the conference room's "hairy wall," which permits illicit peeks through the gaps between its panels. The wall is one of the few overtly suggestive winks that the space makes.

Excerpted from "The Insiders" by Lisa Trollbäck, in *Metropolis*, April 2000.

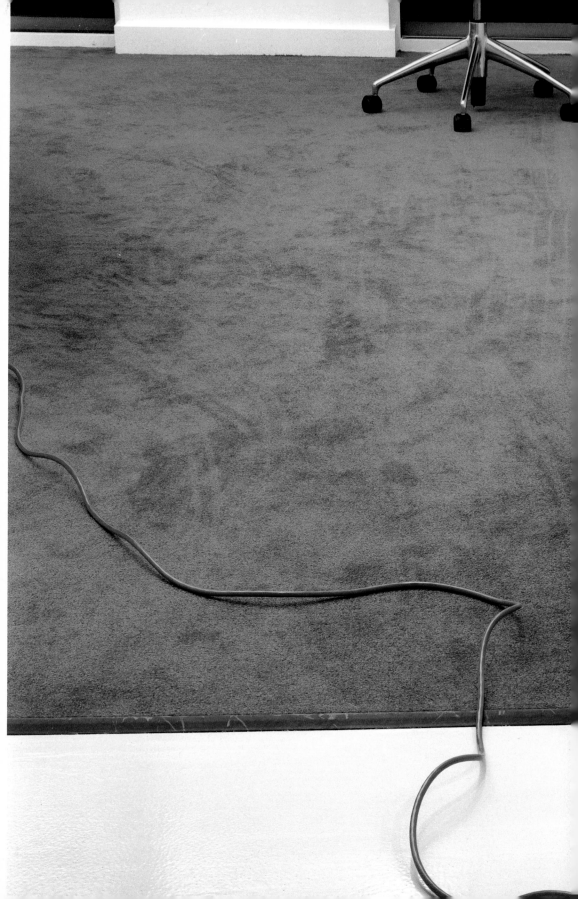

# 19/Split House

SAGAPONAC, LONG ISLAND, NY, 2001

Sagaponac House 22, or the Split House, is designed to accommodate different patterns of contemporary domesticity simultaneously: solitude, work, interaction, and relaxation. Family, guests, and friends, in whatever combination, freely activate the loosely structured house. The main space in the house is the terrace between the two principal volumes of the house, both of which are two stories. The lower level of the structure to the right of the entry steps—containing the garage, a solarium, and outdoor shower—is tucked under the upper-level bedroom and an artist's studio adjacent to a swimming pool.

Opposite, two additional bedrooms occupy the upper level of the second structure, with the main social spaces—kitchen/dining room, living room, screened porch—below. To keep the experience fluid, the "in-between" character of the terrace is repeated on the mezzanine level off the stair of the main house. This mid-level space straddles the private and social realms of the house and provides respite from the main activities of the house. The windows of this room capture the north light and open onto a grove of bamboo.

The house is simply constructed using common materials: wood and steel framing, cement block and stucco walls, and clear wood siding on the upper levels. The house volumes are given generous terraces, providing each room with direct access to the outdoors. Like the Renaissance double house Villa Lante, the emptiness at the center of the house keeps activity—in short, living—as the focus of the house. The raised terrace encourages the use of outdoor space for everything from cooking and dining to sunning and relaxing.

Excerpted from "Sagaponac House 22" in *American Dream: The Houses at Sagaponac. Modern Living in the Hamptons* by Coco Brown. Essays by Richard Meier and Alastair Gordon. New York: Rizzoli International Publications, Inc., 2003.

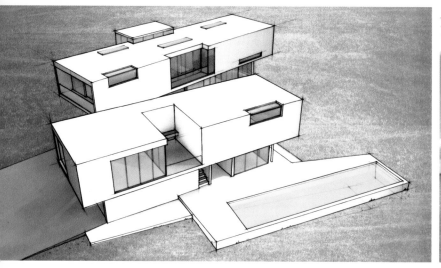

1. Entry
2. Dining Room
3. Kitchen
4. To Powder/Utility Room
5. Living Room
6. Screened Porch
7. Garage
8. Pool Room
9. Pool
10. Sitting Room
11. Terrace
12. Bedroom
13. Master Bedroom
14. Sundeck
15. Guest Bedroom

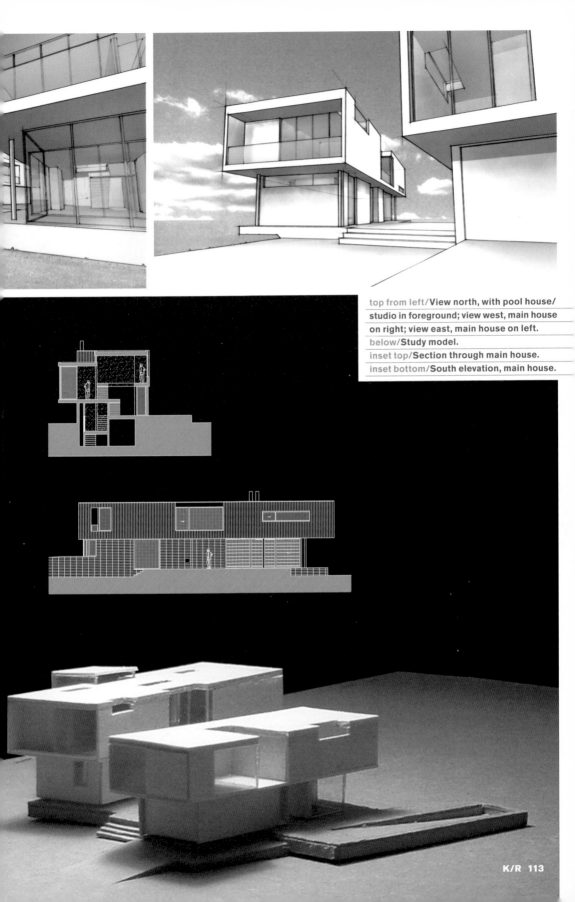

top from left/**View north, with pool house/ studio in foreground; view west, main house on right; view east, main house on left.**
below/**Study model.**
inset top/**Section through main house.**
inset bottom/**South elevation, main house.**

# 20/Court-Houses

DESIGN, K/R AND JOHN BENNETT, MIAMI 2005

While there are many historic precedents for this type of structure, in Mies van der Rohe's studio the "court-house" evolved as a series of glass-enclosed single-story spaces that looked out onto open-air courts and green spaces, all contained compactly within a surrounding rectangular wall. The exterior walls had few or no openings, as the court-houses were intended to be built in clusters.

The Miami court-houses were intended as a field test of Mies's theoretical investigations, which he had never fully concluded in his built work. The plans of the two houses are mirrored along a party wall and frame a fifty-foot live oak that dominated the previously vacant lots in a neighborhood of middle-class cottages built in the 1920s and 30s. The space within the perimeter wall of each unit is approximately 3200 square feet, only half of which is enclosed. Two glass-enclosed pavilions—one with living, dining and kitchen spaces, the other with bedrooms—face each other across a central court. The court itself is divided by a lap pool, which is spanned by a concrete bridge. Two additional open courts, heavily planted, provide alternative perspectives toward the front and the rear of the houses.

The inward orientation of the houses and their fluid interiors provide a sense of spaciousness and privacy unexpected on such a small parcel of land. This phenomenon tends to support Mies's original concept of the court-houses as a cost-effective alterative to the prevalent housing types of the day: free-standing, but expensive, single family houses and low-cost, but spatially uninspiring, row houses and apartment blocks. We saw the great potential of this model.

below/Plan showing two Court-Houses.

opposite page, top/**Living room looking toward front garden.**
opposite page, bottom/**Court at dusk with video projection.**
below/**Bridge over lap pool and bedroom.**

opposite page/**Front garden.**
below/**Dining area with photo mural.**
bottom/**Court facing east.**
following spread/**Street façade of both
Court-Houses.**

# Modern in a
# Post-Modern World
## Terence Riley

When I began working on the exhibition *Mies in Berlin* (Museum of Modern Art, New York, June-September 2001; Barry Bergdoll, co-curator), I did so with a sense that the time was right for another look at the work of Mies van der Rohe. Indeed, the other great figures of the modern movement had already enjoyed a "rehabilitation" of sorts. Major retrospectives of the work of Frank Lloyd Wright, Le Corbusier, Alvar Alto, and Louis Kahn had all demonstrated that the architects' works were never as one-dimensional as the post-modern critics of the 1970s had painted them to be.

The post-modern debate was quite different in those years. While recently post-modernism in architecture has been largely thought to be equivalent to historicism, in the 1970s it was understood to represent a spectrum of attitudes. No event summed up its multivalence as did the first Biennale of Architecture, held in Venice in 1980. The centerpiece of the exhibition was the *Strada Novissma*—literally "the newest street"—which was formed by ten "façades" on each side of the linear gallery, designed by the invited architectural avant-garde of the day. The curator, Paolo Portoghesi, wrote in the foreword to the catalogue, "The return of architecture to the womb of history and its recycling in new syntactic contexts of the traditional forms is one of the symptoms that has produced a profound difference in a series of works and projects in the past few years understood by some critics to be in the ambiguous but efficacious category of post-modern."

Given Portoghesi's emphasis on history, it is not surprising to recall that the *Strada Novissima* included façades by Robert A. M. Stern; Venturi, Rauch, Scott-Brown; Leon Krier; Michael Graves; Ricardo Bofill; Stanley Tigerman; Alan Greenburg; and Thomas Gordon Smith. My own selective memory was jolted, however, when I looked at the catalogue a few years ago and realized the *Strada* also included the work of Rem Koolhaas/OMA, Frank Gehry, Christian de Portzamparc, Hans Hollein, Arata Isozaki, and O. M. Ungers, among others.

The title of Portoghesi's essay was "Against Prohibitionism" and it echoed the arguments for a pluralistic culture of architecture as put forth by Robert Venturi in his seminal book, *Complexity and Contradiction in Architecture* (1966). Whatever "prohibitionism" might mean today, in the 1970s it referred to the orthodoxy that had descended upon modernism as it reached the end of what might be called its natural life. Indeed, the pluralism of the post-modern movement in the 1970s was stitched together by virtue of the fact that its varied protagonists were all "against" something, rather than sharing a common vision. In Portoghesi's essay and the other early post-modern manifestos, one of the common things to be against was Mies. Charles Jencks's plainly contemptuous remarks about the "univalence" of Mies's work were not, despite his rather singular metaphor, unusual for the time: "In the hands of Mies and his disciples this impoverished system has become fetishized to the point where it overwhelms all other concerns (in a similar way the leather boot dominates the shoe fetishist and distracts him from large concerns)."

Indeed, this rather fragile coalition had begun to split apart even before the end of the decade. Philip Johnson, a former devotee of Mies and the subject of another one-man presentation at the 1980 Biennale, wholeheartedly endorsed the historicist wing, if you will, of the post-modern movement. His appearance on the cover of *Time* magazine in 1979, cradling a model of his neo-Chippendale AT&T Building, seriously tipped the balance of power in favor of the traditionalists and set the stage for the acceptance of post-modernism as the official architecture of the 1980s. In that decade we would also see a distinct change in the fascination with history, as the hallmark of post-modernism became not the inventive and interpretive approach to history, such as can be seen in Michael Graves's Portland City Hall, but the archaeologically correct, such as Alan Greenberg's neoclassical works in a strict Georgian style.

Notwithstanding, the 1970s post-modernism coalition would have undoubtedly collapsed under its own weight, with or without Johnson's endorsement of the traditionalists. The year before Johnson appeared on the cover of *Time*, Rem Koolhaas published *Delirious New York: A Retroactive Manifesto for Manhattan*. In the broadest sense of the term, Koolhaas's book was, indeed, an historical argument, although in this case a history seen through the filter of Dali's critical-paranoid method rather than through *The Seven Lamps of Architecture*. It was in that same year that Gehry "deconstructed" his own house in Santa Monica. In the years to come, the left-out wing of the post-modern movement would become increasingly identified as post-structuralist, a term that allied them more strongly with post-modern *philosophy*, leaving the term *post-modern architecture* to the traditionalists.

All this was the backdrop to my own undergraduate and graduate studies in architecture—an education that did not include an extensive exposure to Mies's work. In retrospect, I can see that Mies, who died twelve years before the *Strada Novissima* was staged, had two problems in the post-modern world. He was the *echt* symbol of orthodoxy, based on his search for the universal in architecture. Equally important, however, he was such a towering presence that he remained the symbol of the architectural establishment, even in death. There was no better way to establish your young-Turk credentials than by beating up on Mies. In the experimental mood of the 1970s, power and orthodoxy did not go down well. The only path to new forms of expression for the generation of architects that came of age in the 1970s led around or over Mies. As a student in those times, my peers and I had a slightly different perspective. We could enjoy the heady atmosphere of change without any real idea about what we were all against. I don't think we really knew who Mies was. Latecomers to the revolution by a half-generation, we were sure we were against the architectural aristocrats, but as to any real understanding, we wouldn't have known them if we had seen them.

Inasmuch, I would have to say that my whole awareness of Mies is completely conditioned by post-modernism, in its broadest sense. I literally came to see Mies through post-modern eyes. In the mid-1980s, I was traveling in Europe with the intention of see-ing some of the work of the British architect James Stirling, a key figure of the decade whose work, which combined elements of both historicist and philosophical post-modernism, was noticeably absent from the *Strada Novissima*. Looking up from my map of Berlin, I spotted this enormous black steel canopy supported by giant columns, hovering over a glass cube set up on a granite podium. What is this building? Isn't that Mies? Climbing up to the podium, I walked around it, fairly gawking, until I turned and looked down to see Stirling's building, the *Wissenschaftszentrum*. Hmmmm, very interesting, historical references, skewed geometries, bright colors, very contextual, all the right stuff. Still, I couldn't help but look back admiringly at the Neue Nationalgalerie even though it was all that structural rationalism—heroically abstract, austere, and anticontextual. Walking away, I almost felt guilty realizing that the Stirling building I had gone to see hadn't been nearly as powerful an experience as old modern Mies's steel-and-glass museum.

I can't say that I underwent a conversion or that Mies became some sort of a permanent fixation, although my interest did grow over time. The next scene in this story was Barcelona, the site of Mies's landmark German Pavilion for the 1929 Universal Exposition, which had been dismantled after the fair closed. Until it was reconstructed in the 1980s—a post-modern event in and of itself—it was the most famous building that almost no one had ever seen. Mies knew that it was his best work in Europe but virtually no one else did. Its plan and the existing black-and-white photographs of it became textbook images in the literal sense. The architecture was literally bound between the covers of history books. After seeing the reconstruction, I finally understood how wide a gap existed between the actual architecture and those historical photographs depicting Mies striding away in a black top hat as the King of Spain drives off in a Hispano-Suiza.

The Neue Nationalgalerie was Mies's last project and, despite its location, it represented his architectural values at the end of nearly thirty years in the United States. While see-ing it reminded me of the power of those ideas, seeing the German Pavilion made me consider how utterly different it was from Mies's later work. First was the color. I was not quite ready for Mies in color: red, green, yellow-orange, all reflected in glass—some if it slightly gray, some of it slightly green, some of it clear, some of it milk white—chrome, and water. Whereas Mies had been severely criticized by the post-modernists for his austerity, the pavilion is about as sensual as an inanimate object can be.

Mies was also criticized for his later use of universal and minimally abstract planning devices such as the grid, and there is no question that a building like the Neue National-galerie is a classical example of this strategy. Robert Venturi, claiming "Less is a bore," instead turned to the contingent and the contextual, citing historic Rome as an example of a desired complexity. Curious, then, it was to discover that the paving grid of the German Pavilion did not determine the location of all of the columns or the partition walls, which, rather, shifted on and off the grid to some kind of boogie rhythm that I have never been able to figure out. Then again, maybe there is no reason, at least no more reason than choreography has a reason. (By the way, in his on-camera interview with filmmaker Michael Blackwood, released in 1988, Venturi said the only words he regret-ted from *Complexity and Contradiction* were those paraphrasing Mies.)

Not surprisingly, Mies's work in the United States was characterized as being the essence of structural rationalism by both post-modernists and post-structuralists. But how structurally rational is it to have columns clad in mirror-finish chrome, columns that reflect the sky or mimic the surrounding materials? Recalling the fascination that the surrealists, whose work Mies knew very well, had with mirrors, can this really be called a rational—much less structurally rational—work of architecture?

Mies's supposed objectivity was also a target of both post-modern and post-structuralist critics who took aim at the dreaded "glass box," the purported architecture of nothingness that perspective invented. What struck me when I visited the German Pavilion, however, was not the use of glass as an abstract anti-material but the actual physical qualities of the glass—or, I should say the many types and colors of glass and their effects. Still, I felt these effects must be some sort of serendipitous byproduct of some other more rational goal. An unfinished rendering of the interior of the pavilion in the Mies archive, however, demonstrates otherwise. Seeing the various differences in shading, it is evident that Mies didn't think of the glass as simply transparent but as a kind of screen that mediates your perception of the space as light passes through it. In other words, the strange and beautiful perceptual effects of the collage of glass surfaces and reflective surfaces were carefully explored by Mies and were in fact the point of the design.

The literary critic Jean Starobinski wrote an essay about the "subjective gaze," the more personal and emotive aspect of visual experience, balancing the rationalism of so-called objective vision. The title of the essay, "Poppea's Veil," refers to a courtesan in ancient Rome who adopted the practice of wearing a veil over her face to make herself more alluring. In the words of Starobinski, "The hidden fascinates….Obstacle and interposed sign, Poppea's veil engenders a perfection that is immediately stolen away, and by its very flight demands to be recaptured by our desire." Where objective vision is supposed to be detached and rational, Starobinski is referring to a scenario where the "veil" creates a relationship between the viewer of a female nude and the thing seen, the object of desire. In the pavilion, George Kolbe's sculpture, *The Dawn*, at the end of the long diagonal axis that organizes the interlocking spaces of the pavilion, might be seen as Poppea and the architecture as her veils. Seen from afar, through various shimmering veils, the visitor is drawn toward the statue but is repeatedly turned away by the free-floating partitions.

Is it too much to project this kind of contemporary discourse on Mies's early twentieth-century work? Apparently not, as even historical black-and-white photographs demonstrate a struggle to capture these shimmering visual sensations and transient reflections without the benefit of more revealing color film. These images and others clearly portray the way in which the viewers became enmeshed in the architectural surfaces—the viewer became the viewed—the essence of the subjective condition.

The reflection of the Kolbe statue, appearing as a kind of collage element on the more abstract surfaces, was an equally powerful attraction to the eye of the photographer. It should not be overlooked that these images are not without their own biases, typical of the time. Rosemary Bletter wrote an essay for the *Mies in Berlin* catalogue entitled "Mies and Dark Transparency," in which she sees the Kolbe statue, as well as the sculpted female figures in Mies's 1929 Glass Room, 1931 Exhibition house, and—by extension—Ms. Farnsworth in her Mies-designed house, as being entrapped.

Still, it is ironic that the pavilion is more about surface than about structure, more about the skin—both suggested by the sculptural nude and the architectural surfaces—than about bones. Things that are about surface are typically referred to as being superficial—having "skin-deep beauty." I came to realize, however, that the pavilion embodied "deep-skin beauty."

If a new generation of architects has rediscovered the glass box it would probably be less of a surprise to Mies than to Jencks and other writers that predicted the demise of his influence. However, I think that it is also safe to say that the interest of a newer generation in recognizably Miesian themes is not—and could not be—rooted in the same values that we have come to associate with him or his work.

Indeed, I think it is evident that an even younger generation is attracted to Mies's work for reasons that Mies would have never understood. The Farnsworth House, like most of Mies's residential projects, may have been radical in terms of its architectural expression but is essentially a traditionally conceived country residence in the Virgilian mode. Like Palladio's villas, it is essentially a platform for contemplation, a viewing point from which the occupant can look out on nature. At the time of its construction, a well-known controversy broke out about the extent to which Mies's vision conflicted with traditional American values regarding privacy and, unsaid in all the fuss, modesty in architecture. *The House Beautiful* crowd raged about the ability for passersby to look in—wherever those passersby were supposed to come from in a remote part of Plano, Illinois, is not clear—but a distinct undertone can be heard: Who is the middle-aged, unmarried woman doctor and why would she ever put herself in a glass house anyway?

Still, the feminist critique of Mies deserves its hearing and after reading Alice Friedman's and Bletter's essays on the female form in Mies's glass structures, I do see the photograph of the model of the house in a different way. I think it is equally clear, however, that the debate in the mid-1950s about public and private no longer holds the same weight. If the rebuilt German Pavilion has made a mark on contemporary designers, the Farnsworth house has also found new echoes in the work of younger architects. Scott Cohen's Torus House literally transforms the white steel pavilion in the landscape, fusing Mies's sense of the boundless horizon with an internalized sense of the seamless and continuous. Like the Farnsworth house, Cohen is relying on the remoteness of the Torus House to insure the occupant's privacy, which—despite the criticism of the Farnsworth house—was a value of great importance to Mies. The extent to which contemporary designers have played with the limits of the divide between public and private would, no doubt, have scandalized Mies. Shigeru Ban's Curtain Wall House, the title of which is itself a play on words about Meisian themes, is essentially a three-story Farnsworth House sited not in rural Illinois but in the center of Tokyo. The triple-height curtains are reminiscent of shoji, traditional lightweight Japanese sliding screens, but they are equally reminiscent of stage curtains.

Mack Scogin and Merrill Elam's house in Atlanta similarly flirts with the limits of conventional ideas of privacy and its corollary—modesty. The second-floor master bedroom is clearly visible through the panes of glass that separate it from the lap pool just outside. Contrary to expectation, this is not the rear of the house but the front. A panel of frosted glass on the pool's outer edge provides a minimal screen between passersby and the house's owners: the husband and wife can lounge in the pool and overhear comments about how ugly the house is.

In these projects, the interest in breaking down barriers between the public and private focuses on the skin of the building. Like Poppea's veil, the skin mediates a relationship between the two. In my view, the new popularity of the glass box lies therein, the glass house has come to be seen as interactive—a concept with which Mies would have no way to relate—an architectural analog to the connectivity so desired in a mediated world.

This position becomes more evident in those projects in which the architects intermingle the physical interaction of viewer and viewed in the glass pavilion with virtual interactivity. A project by a Japanese architect submitted for the competition for "Another Glass House," sponsored by a Japanese publishing house in 1991, rhetorically transforms the icon of contemplation, the Zen rock garden at Ryo-anji, into a vision of contemporary techno-domesticity. Walls of monitors provide surrogate windows, displacing time and distance.

The Kyle Residence by Joel Sanders similarly takes the Meisian glass house as a point of departure. An astro-turf lawn turned up perpendicularly to screen out neighbors competes with digital projections of artificial nature. Bernard Tschumi takes yet another tack; his Video Pavilion at Groenigen is literally a glass house—structure as well as skin— where the interspersed video monitors create an endlessly reflective environment, intermingling viewer and the viewed, now technically expressed.

Perhaps the most exciting recent iteration of this theme draws upon both the Barcelona Pavilion and the Farnsworth House as sources. The Kramlich House by Herzog & de Meuron, as originally designed, was meant for a site in Napa, California, for collectors of video and multimedia art. The proposed structure reflected the tripartite organization of the Neue Nationalgalerie with an enclosed subterranean level (for video projections) and open main level (where video projections on the partitions are collaged onto views of nature) and a roof terrace for distant views. In essence, the section sandwiches a new vision of the world—part "real," part "virtual"—between the purely artificial below and the purely natural above.

I think that all of these recent projects have a common point of reference: that is, the work of Mies van der Rohe as it has come to be seen in recent years. Unlike the New York Five, for example, with their obvious and self-acknowledged debt to a common source, Le Corbusier, it seems that Mies's name was, until recently, one that still could not be invoked. In the work of Rem Koolhaas/OMA, however, increasingly frank references to Mies's work have been evident for many years. The House in Bordeaux is a good example. It is hard to see the principal elevation—photographed from below, the upper story hovering over a long retaining wall—without thinking of Mies's first project, the Riehl House, completed in 1907. Similarly, the elevation from the garden recalls Mies's seminal sketch for a glass house on a hillside, a solitary sketch that has nonetheless had numerous incarnations in the work of Charles Eames, Philip Johnson, and many others.

Rem Koolhaas's bulky manifesto, *S, M, L, XL*, is notable for many reasons, not least of all for its specific references to Mies in the author's discourse on modernism and the architectural present. In the first chapter, two of Mies's projects, the Barcelona Pavilion and the Kroller-Muller Villa, serve as prologue to a presentation of OMA's House for Two Friends, the Fukuoka Housing project, and the Villa d'Ava.

Reflecting his generation's difficulty in coming to terms with the power architect of the previous generation, Koolhaas's presentation of Mies is a conflicted one. No other architect's work figures so prominently in the book, but Koolhaas's tone is more Oedipal than honorific. His revisionist and intentionally provocative interpretation of the Barcelona Pavilion, the most modern of architectural icons, is complete, presenting a vision of Mies that is no longer pure, classical, and sober but unexpectedly Delirious Hollywood. Koolhaas further describes Mies's project as, "bent"—a term that refers to the photocopy distortion of the plan that appears in the book but which is synonymous with "queer" as well. No longer an object trapped in a distant, unreachable, or perfect-ible past, the Barcelona Pavilion has been reworked for current consumption: The image of a buff athlete showering in Koolhaas's House for Two Friends is what would be called in the film industry a "remake" of George Kolbe's cast bronze maiden captured within the Pavilion's courtyard reflecting pool. Koolhaas's text makes it clear that his genera-tion's interest in Mies is not to be seen as a renewed interest in the post-war corporate architectural culture of the 1960s but in a fundamental reconfiguration of Mies's work in the imagination of contemporary architects.

The work of a Spanish artist, Iñigo Manglano-Ovalle, epitomizes, in my mind, the generational shift in perceptions of Mies's work. Not as angry as Koolhaas—whose architecture is always influenced by his consciousness of his role within the generation of 1968—Manglano-Ovalle's large-scale video and photography project, entitled *Le Baiser (The Kiss)* is more literally touching. The artist documents a window washer cleaning the Farnsworth House from the exterior as a young woman works at a computer within, expressing all of the issues raised here—interactivity, desire, technology, subjec-tivity, and their relationship to an architecture of surfaces. As the squeegee "kisses" the skin of the house, the window washer and the woman carry on a flirtation from either side of the glass. The difference between this contemporary vision of Mies's work and Mies's own is, of course, the difference of a new generation.

Nonetheless, I have to admit to being very surprised at the popular and critical reception of *Mies in Berlin*. A quarter-million people passed through MoMA's galleries and the media's reaction was nearly exclusively favorable. I had hoped for, at best, a good contro-versy, a raging debate—not a love-fest. I think that the exhibition not only confirmed the relevance, even popularity, of modernism in a post-modern world but also pointed to a popular disaffection with post-modern architecture, at least the historic variety.

If this proves to be true, I think that it will confirm, to a certain extent, that the post-modern/post-structuralist critique of the 1970s and 1980s had achieved its goals and even outlived its purpose. Indeed, it seems that renewed interest in the search for the modern in the post-modern world is proportionate to the extent to which contemporary architects have internalized the post-modern criticisms of late international style architecture—its banality, sterility, and aloofness, in short, its irrelevance as a cultural practice.

The "renewed adherence to the spirit of the age," as Tony Vidler put it, might also be traced to the failure of post-modernism's goal of restoring not traditional architecture but traditional cities. The public, never as ideological as architects might think, broadly supported historicist rhetoric not, in my opinion, because they were committed to traditional architecture but because the promise of the restoration of pre-modern cities—and with it the promise of a life free of modern angst and full of traditional values—was particularly resonant. Only in highly controlled circumstances, such as Disney's planned community of Celebration, Florida, has the urban dimension of post-modernism been physically realized, to, it should be noted, very mixed reviews. Indeed, the messiness of contemporary culture has been highly resistant to the type of control required to re-create traditional urban forms and the general public has been highly selective in its commitment to post-modern ideals. Perhaps we have come to the point where we would prefer to be something else but we realize we can't. We realize that what we are, in essence, is modern in a post-modern world.

# The Architects' Room
## Terence Riley

The term *tectonics* is derived from the Greek and refers literally to the "poetry of building." That such a thing might exist may be surprising to some, as would the underlying supposition that something as pragmatic as construction might have any voice at all.

In considering the source of this voice, it is interesting to note one of the more prevalent ways, in Western culture, of indicating the status of an architect. In Germany, a professional is said to be a member of the *Architektenkammer*, the architects' chamber. The same terminology, in various translations, is used in numerous other European societies. To be admitted to the architects' chamber—or, more simply, the architects' room—suggests an exclusive realm of the initiated, distinguished from outsiders by the specificity of their knowledge.

That architects, as a group, would develop a specific language to match the specificity of their work is unsurprising. More to the point, however, is how this language has come to absorb associated ideas with unexpectedly broad implication. The platonic circle twice bisected creates four ninety-degree angles, each known as a right angle. The rightness of the angle refers to a whole cluster of concepts more metaphysical than material: correctness, legitimacy, and so on. In the same linguistic vein, the term "wright" refers to one who has mastered a skill, as in wainwright or wheelwright. In yet another instance, milled steel or lumber that is free from warping and other dimensional defects is referred to as true.

Despite the implications of these broader philosophical issues in the language of tectonics, a distinction must be made between these concepts and notions of tautologies or orthodoxies. Indeed, poetry in construction requires, as it would in any written language, a certain level of nuance and subjectivity. Evidence of such a conditional nature exists in yet another architectural term, tolerance, which refers to acceptable deviations in the form, dimensions, or surface qualities of a construction. A more slippery term might also be introduced here, fabrication, which jumps between the negative sense of a falsehood and the more neutral sense of the process, or product, of making.

Perhaps no other architect in this century understood the conditional nature of correctness in building as did Ludwig Mies van der Rohe, the son of a stonecutter without formal training in architecture. Mies's application of I-beams to the exterior of the Seagram Building has been criticized as a mere formal gesture, with negligible structural or functional value. Yet the same could be said of *metopes*, the sculpted rectangular elements placed rhythmically in the cornices of ancient Greek buildings. Within the language of architecture they achieve the same goal: the fabric of the structure speaks poetically of itself. The metopes recall the unfinished, exposed butt ends of the timber roof rafters of older Greek architecture, and in a similar fashion the applied I-beams refer to the structural steel lattice wrapped behind the curtain wall.

If these formal devices might be said to reveal certain aspects of the building not other-wise apparent, there exists a more direct relationship between the term reveal—referring to the slight gap that separates various elements of a construction—and the language of architecture. A reveal uncovers the processes and defines the materials of its own making. An elegant example of this idea of revelation in contemporary architecture might be seen in Peter Zumthor's Kunsthaus in Bregenz, Austria. Eloquently demonstrating that fabrication can transcend the mundane, the museum is a complex interweaving of its inner concrete shell and outer glazed skin. The typical insulated-glass curtain wall is completely rethought and expanded into a visible expression of its various components: an external skin of translucent glass shingles, which acts as a light filter and heat shield; a one-meter-deep interstitial space, which acts as a thermal barrier; and transparent clerestory glazing, which brings the filtered light into a plenum of space above each of the four levels of galleries. The carefully calculated shingling of the outer skin serves to reveal rather than conceal this complexity.

As a way of exploring the possibilities of techtonic expression, four architectural installa-tions in the Abby Aldrich Rockefeller Sculpture Garden at The Museum of Modern Art, New York, were conceived by four individual architects or teams following mutual discussions and analyses of the site (*Fabrications*, January-April, 1998). As a group, the four installations revealed not only certain aspects of their materials and construction but also various aspects of the site and its specific context. Like the full-scale fragments in a Beaux-Arts museum, the installations were seen as having an intrinsic aesthetic dimension as well as a didactic one: Each of the pieces also engaged broader issues, speaking to individual concerns.

Of all the activities in the repertoire of construction, glazing (installation and fitting of a building's glass surfaces) is most closely associated with the twentieth century and the philosophical and architectural issues that defined it. The installation by Henry Smith-Miller and Laurie Hawkinson (Smith-Miller + Hawkinson Architects) transformed the glass and steel International Style façade of Philip Johnson's 1964 East Wing, with its clearly defined separation between structure and skin, by literally and philosophically "building upon it." The classical framed view that it created—not so different from, say, peering out from between the columns of the Parthenon—suggested a universal per-spective, an objective and unchanging view of the world.

In Smith-Miller and Hawkinson's construction, various aspects of the East Wing façade were reconsidered and reconfigured. The relationship between the black steel piers and the transparent glass panes was inverted; a new glass pier acted as a sup-port and the dark hue of the skeletal structure was extended into the building as a series of planar surfaces. Furthermore, the classical sense of spatial continuity was challenged by a series of folded plates that rose up from the floor of Johnson's East Wing and seemingly passed through the glass façade, becoming the installation's metaphorical, rather than universal, horizon. The relationship between vision and structure was also challenged: A dark panel obscured the view from one section of the Johnson façade, replacing it with a digital view of the site landscape projected into the building's interior.

Alfred Munkenbeck and Stephen Marshall's (Munkenbeck + Marshall Architects) minimal shelter consisted of a canopy supported by three slender columns with an infill of woven steel mats on two sides. The canopy hovered over the bridge that spanned the eastern reflecting pool of the Sculpture Garden, creating an assemblage of new and preexisting parts. In its spare, essential form, the structure recalled the underlying Miesian influences on Johnson's design of the garden. Yet, upon closer inspection, other influences could have been noted. The nineteenth-century German theorist Gottfried Semper suggested a model of the primitive hut as an early source of architecture. Semper's hut consisted of a base stone, which rooted the structure and provided a suitable surface for the hearth. Atop the stone base, Semper imagined, rose the timber frame structure of the walls and the roof, which were then infilled by woven materials, unifying masonry, carpentry, and weaving, each used in the most effective way. In Munkenbeck and Marshall's shelter, the stone hearth gave way to a stone bridge and the household fire was replaced by the image of water. Semper's structure suggested a kind of cosmic connection between the earthbound masonry below, the lighter framework above, and the skyward trail of the smoke from the hearth through the peak of the roof. While there remained a dialogue between the frame structure and the woven infill material, there was a definite shift from the vertical *axis mundi*. As the water below and the canopy above were both reflective, the space between became a slice connecting the celestial and the mundane, with light coming in from above and below simultaneously.

The installation by Enrique Norten and Guy Nordenson (TEN Arquitectos) consisted of a glass structure situated in a paved, open area of the garden. Beneath the structure's glass canopy, the garden's two-by-four-foot marble paving slabs had been removed, revealing the rubble of the townhouses that formerly occupied the site. Distinctly recalling the architecture of an archaeological site, the installation restored the memory of the previous construction to the current conditions. Standing below the canopy and upon the rubble, the viewer experienced a shift in physical, as well as historical, point of view. As if to confirm the notions of relative permanence and transience previously mentioned, the bricks of the Beaux-Arts townhouse were transformed into a subsurface sedimentary layer. This installation also reminded us that a new fabrication might be made by the removal or displacement, rather than the addition, of material. As evidenced by such projects as Michael Heizer's earthworks or Gordon Matta-Clark's excisions of architectural fragments, such operations can have profound effects on the natural landscape. In a densely built environment, the effects are no less profound. As this type of environment will characterize the twenty-first century, perhaps more than any other, Norten's installation spoke of the future as much as the past.

The installation by Monica Ponce de Leon and Nader Tehrani (Office dA) was a relatively lightweight, transient structure with multiple references, made entirely of sheet steel. The material was subjected to a number of transformative operations traditionally associated with metalworking, each calculated with the assistance of computer analysis: perforation, which reduced its weight; milling the surface to produce a texture; and bending and folding, which gave it a form of structural stability. In this instance, the form resembled a cascading staircase, suggesting the amount of strength imparted to the otherwise relatively weak sheet material. Folding and bending techniques were also used to assemble the various sections of the installation, interlocking them in the manner of large shingles.

While the installation suggested the form of a stair, it was also a self-supporting canopy that rested against the bulk of the eighteen-foot-high masonry wall that formed the northern edge of the sculpture garden. The metalwork here, unlike that in other types of canopies, was continuous and not divided into structural and nonstructural members; rather, a different type of contrast was suggested.

The juxtaposition of the masonry and the metalwork underscored their fundamental differences and recalled the experimental house projects of the French architect Jean Prouvé, particularly the projects exhibited in the 1951 Exposition des arts ménagers in Paris. In that unbuilt scheme, a masonry wall was to be the spine of the house, and factory-produced curved metal sections were to rest against it, creating the interior space. In both the Prouvé project and Office dA installation, the qualities of the masonry—heavy, massive, site built, permanent—are played off the qualities of the metalwork—lightweight, perforated, factory built, transportable.

In each of these four "fabrications," there was a revelation or, as Heidegger would have said, an "unconcealment." The rightness or truthfulness of these works derived not from a conception of orthodoxy, but from the art of fabrication.

# Light Construction
## Terence Riley

In recent years, a new architectural sensibility has emerged, one that not only reflects the distance of our culture from the machine aesthetic of the early twentieth century but also marks a fundamental shift in emphasis after three decades during which debate about architecture focused on issues of form. In projects notable for artistic and technical innovation, contemporary designers are investigating the nature and potential of architectural surfaces. They are concerned not only with their visual and material qualities but with the meanings they may convey. Influenced by aspects of our culture including electronic media and the computer, architects and artists are rethinking the interrelationships of architecture, visual perception, and structure.

Discussed in this essay are some thirty contemporary projects, created in response to commissions and competitions in ten countries. As the great majority of these works have been built, they engage their environments on material as well as theoretical levels. This essay situates the projects in a broad, synthetic context, addressing both their cultural and aesthetic dimensions. Priority is given to the viewer's visual encounter with a structure, a choice that is not meant to imply a rigid hierarchy of importance but to recognize that the appearance of architecture provides not only the initial but also frequently the most defining contribution toward its eventual comprehension.

The sensibility expressed in these projects refers, but does not return, to the visual objectivity embraced by many early modernists, particularly as it is expressed in their fascination with glass structures. Ludwig Hilberseimer's 1929 essay "*Glasarchitektur*" represents that rationalist outlook and serves as a historical antipode to contemporary attitudes. For Hilberseimer, the use of glass in architecture furthers hygienic and economic goals; he discusses its formal properties only insofar as they enable the architect to express the structural system more clearly. Aesthetic concerns are essentially negated. He argues:

> Glass is all the fashion today. Thus it is used in ways that are frequently preposterous, having nothing to do with functional but only formal and decorative purposes, to call attention to itself; and the result, grotesquely, is that very often glass is combined with the load-bearing structure in a way that glass's characteristic effects of lightness and transparency become completely lost.[1]

Hilberseimer's *sachlich* approach contains its own understated implications for an aesthetic vision. Describing the Crystal Palace (London, 1850–51), which "for the first time showed the possibilities of iron and glass structures," Hilberseimer writes, "It obliterated the old opposition of light and shadow, which had formed the proportions of past architecture. It made a space of evenly distributed brightness; it created a room of shadowless light."[2] The extensive use in contemporary architecture of semitransparent glazing materials (such as frosted or mottled glass), translucent plastic sheathings, double layers of glass (which, even if clear, produce enough reflections to function as screens), and an apparently infinite number of perforated materials, results in spaces very different from Hilberseimer's "room of shadowless light." Indeed, recent projects point to the possibility that "transparency" can also express the shadows of architecture.

The literary critic Jean Starobinski begins his essay "Poppaea's Veil" with this state-ment: "The hidden fascinates."[3] His title refers to a passage in Montaigne's essay, "That difficulty increases desire" (II: 15), in which the philosopher examines a complicated relationship between Poppaea, who was Nero's mistress, and her admirers: "How did Poppaea hit on the idea of hiding the beauties of her face behind a mask if not to make them more precious to her lovers?"[4] Starobinski analyzes the veil: "Obstacle and interposed sign, Poppaea's veil engenders a perfection that is immediately stolen away, and by its very flight demands to be recaptured by our desire."[5] To describe the action of the viewer, Starobinski rejects the term *vision*, which implies an immediately penetrat-ing certitude, in favor of *gaze*: "If one looks at the etymology, one finds that to denote directed vision French resorts to the word *regard* [gaze], whose root originally referred not to the act of seeing but to expectation, concern, watchfulness, consideration, and safeguard."[6] Starobinski's metaphor is literary, but it easily translates into architectural terms: The façade becomes an interposed veil, triggering a subjective relationship by distancing the viewer of the building from the space or forms within and isolating the viewer within from the outside world.

Created by streams of water running over light-gauge metal fencing in frigid weather, Michael Van Valkenburgh's elegantly simple Radcliffe Ice Walls (Cambridge, MA, 1988) gives the metaphor substance: Like Poppaea's veil, the walls interpose between the viewer and the landscape an ephemeral material (a frozen cloud) and an image (the fence) signifying protection or obstacle. Another germane example is the Ghost House by Philip Johnson (New Canaan, CT, 1985), also made of chain link fencing, which recalls both Frank Gehry's buildings made from off-the-shelf materials and Robert Irwin's diaphanous landscape projects. This minimalist rendition of the archetypal house was designed as a nursery, a latter-day lath house, for growing flowers. The chain-link surfaces not only render the house and its interior as a spectral form, but also prevent foraging deer or other inquisitive visitors from reaching the flowerbeds—a most succinct representation of Poppaea's distanced perfection, a literal expression of the watchful and concerned gaze.

A similarly mediated relationship between the viewer and a distanced space within can be seen in larger, more complex projects, such as the Saishunkan Seiyaku Women's Dormitory by Kazuyo Sejima (Kumamoto, Japan, 1991). The dormitory's heavily screened façades, finely perforated like a sieve, provide maximum blockage with the fewest hints of the interior spaces. Inside, these spaces are relatively free and open, with light filtering through the façades and descending from above. Still, various screened materials used throughout the project impose physical limitations on the vision of passersby. Like a Russian doll, the spaces nest one inside another, further and further removed from the viewer's grasp.

In these projects and others, the distance created between the viewer and the space within suggests, on some level, a voyeuristic condition made explicit in a gymnasium designed by Charles Thanhauser and Jack Esterson (New York City, 1993). In place of typical locker rooms for showering and changing are four freestanding cubicles within the training area, partially enclosed in frosted glass. From various perspectives, the obscured images of athletes dressing and undressing can be observed, accentuating the sensual aspects of physical culture. As in Alfred Hitchcock's *Rear Window*, the anonymity and detachment of the images enhance sensuality; in Montaigne's words, they "entrap our desires and ... attract us by keeping us at a distance."[7]

That all the preceding projects might be referred to as "transparent" suggests a new-found interest in a term long associated with the architecture of the modern movement. Yet the tension between viewer and object implied by the use of architectural façade as a veiling membrane indicates a departure from past attitudes and a need to reexamine the word *transparency* as it relates to architecture. The presence of a new attitude is confirmed by a brief glance at such projects as the Goetz Collection by Jacques Herzog and Pierre de Meuron (Munich, 1992), the Cartier Foundation for Contemporary Art by Jean Nouvel (Paris, 1994), or the ITM Building by Toyo Ito (Matsuyama, Japan, 1993). The Goetz Collection, whose supporting structure is enclosed between the frosted surfaces of a double-glass façade, appears ghost-like, a complete reversal of the structural clarity of the so-called Miesian glass box. Seen through a freestanding, partially glazed palisade, the frame structure of the Cartier Foundation is more explicit and the use of clear plate glass more extensive than in the Goetz Collection. Even so, the Cartier Foundation achieves visual complexity—"haze and evanescence" in the words of the architect—due to the overlapping buildup of views and multiple surface reflections. Transparency in the ITM building and the Cartier Foundation is not created simply by applying a glass curtain wall to the exterior of the building's frame. Rather, the idea of transparency is present deep within the structures; one seems to be suspended within multiple layers of transparency, not only vertical wall surfaces but horizontal surfaces such as the translucent floor panels of Nouvel's project and the reflective floor and ceiling materials of the ITM Building. About the latter, the critic Yoshiharu Tsukamoto has noted: "The result is an interior bleached of all sense we customarily associate with the materials, sublimated into an experience of 'weightlessness,' in Ito's own terminology."[8]

Hilberseimer's ideal of shadowless light is difficult to discern in the banal office towers and residential blocks erected in the postwar building boom. The depredations of the debased International Style of those years provided fertile ground for critics of both the modern rationalists and their latter-day followers. The antipathy of the architectural historian Colin Rowe for the kind of architecture proposed by Hilberseimer was but-tressed by a distaste for the technological, anticlassical ethos of the glass curtain wall, which he felt was bereft of the intellectual complexities to be found in the traditional façade. In his critique of the purported objectivity of the early modern rationalists, Rowe found an ally in the painter Robert Slutsky, a former student of Josef Albers. Slutsky's interest in Gestalt psychology had led him to question the claims to objectivity of some modern painters. In 1955–56, Rowe and Slutsky co-wrote the essay "Transparency:

Literal and Phenomenal," which was first published in 1963 and was widely read, influencing several generations of American architects. In it they state: "[The observer] may enjoy the sensation of looking through a glass wall and thus be able to see the interior and the exterior of the building simultaneously; but, in doing so, he will be conscious of few of those equivocal emotions which derive from phenomenal transparency."[9] They propose "phenomenal transparency" as an abstract, theoretical sense of transparency derived from skillful formal manipulation of the architectural façade, viewed frontally, as opposed to the more straightforward "literal transparency" that they ascribe to the curtain-wall architecture of the modern rationalists.

Rem Koolhaas's 1989 Bibliothèque Nationale de France project—a massive, glass-enclosed cubic structure—offers a kind of transparency that appears to fall entirely outside Rowe and Slutzky's scheme: a building with the visual complexity they sought, which nevertheless rejects the traditional façade that Rowe ultimately defended. It is a building in which transparency is conceived, in the words of the architectural historian Anthony Vidler, "as a solid, not a void, with the interior volumes carved out of a crystalline block so as to float within it, in amoebic suspension. These are then represented on the surface of the cube as shadowy presences, their three-dimensionality displayed ambiguously and flattened, superimposed on one another in a play of amorphous densities." Vidler, taking us a step further toward understanding the new direction of contemporary architecture, also writes: "The subject is suspended in a difficult moment between knowledge and blockage."[10]

The visual experience described by Vidler is certainly not the type that Rowe and Slutsky disparage as literal. But does the viewer's ambiguous perception of the building's interior volumes evoke those "equivocal emotions" that derive, Rowe and Slutsky argue, from phenomenal transparency? The word *ambiguous* plays an important role both in Rowe and Slutzky's writings and in the more recent ones of Vidler; but it is not enough to think that all things ambiguous are necessarily related. The distinction between the experience of Koolhaas's design, as Vidler describes it, and the terms of analysis proposed by Rowe and Slutzky can be best understood if we look to the passage in which they use paintings by Pablo Picasso and Georges Braque to provide a "prevision," as they call it, of literal and phenomenal transparency.[11] They see Picasso's *Man with a Clarinet* of 1911 as an example of literal transparency, "a positively transparent figure standing in a relatively deep space." Braque's *The Portuguese* of the same year reverses this experience: The painting's "highly developed interlacing of horizontal and vertical gridding ... establishes a primarily shallow space."

At this point it seems necessary to separate Rowe from Slutsky, whose concerns led him into a deep investigation of the relationship between the fine arts and the psychology of perception.[12] While admiring Slutzky's analysis, Rowe ultimately is concerned with how the cubist paintings might support his conviction that modern architecture represents nothing more than a formal evolution out of, rather then a break with, the architecture of the classical past. Disregarding the fundamental differences between traditional perspectival construction and synthetic cubism—and setting aside for the moment the differences between *Man with a Clarinet* and *The Portuguese*—we can identify three aspects of these paintings that made them useful to Rowe for architectural analysis: their frontality, analogous to that of the traditional façade; their figure-ground relationships, which privileged formal discernment; and their synthetic spatial depth, which suggested to Rowe an affinity with the compositional elements of the classical orders. Thus, the analytical tools developed by Slutzky to undermine rationalist objectivity in painting, ironically, serve Rowe to defend the objective viewpoint of the architectural connoisseur. In an extended comparison of Gropius's Bauhaus workshop wing, displaying "literal transparency," and Le Corbusier's Villa Garches, representing phenomenal transparency, Rowe and Slutzky even criticize Gropius for "relying on the diagonal viewpoint," rather than the fixed, axial viewpoint of Le Corbusier's work and, for that matter, the canvases of Picasso and Braque.[13] In so doing, they continue, Gropius "has exteriorized the opposed movements of his space, has allowed them to flow away into infinity."

Regardless of their ultimate positions, Rowe and Slutzky's ideas about transparency rest on the premise that the viewer has visual access to the object directly within a perspective field or by constructing a visual path through the shallow space of the Cubist grid. Vidler's term *blockage* has no function in a discussion of penetrating the spaces created by Picasso and Braque (or Rowe's architectural exemplar, Le Corbusier), but the term strongly resonates with the work of Marcel Duchamp, particularly his *Large Glass* of 1915–23. For Duchamp the surface of the *Large Glass* is a kind of threshold, distinct from the object itself, suggesting a subjective tension between the viewer and object like that created by Poppaea's veil; it is to be "looked at rather than through," in the words of the architecture critic Kenneth Frampton.[14] Another way of describing the effect on the viewer is suggested by Octavio Paz: Whereas Picasso's work represents "movement before painting," Paz explains that "right from the start Duchamp set up a vertigo of delay in opposition to the vertigo of acceleration. In one of the notes in the celebrated *Green Box* he writes, 'use *delay* instead of "picture" or "painting"; "picture on glass" becomes "delay in glass." ' "[15]

Frampton's comments on the *Large Glass* are made in an essay in which he compares Duchamp's great work to Pierre Chareau's Maison de Verre (Paris, 1932), a long-neglected masterpiece of prewar architecture, which ran completely against the grain of modern rationalist thought. It was sheathed in layers of transparent and translucent materials, which alternately obscured and revealed a sequence of views–"Ambiguous characteristics," Frampton notes, which "would surely have been anathema to the fresh air and hygiene cult of the mainstream modern movement."[16] Though the glass architecture of the Maison de Verre might have been dismissed by the rationalist Hilberseimer, it remains resistant to the visual delectation espoused by Rowe. Frampton points out that it served as both a private residence and gynecologist's office, a combination of functions richly analogous to the division of the *Large Glass* into the Bride's domain above and that of the eroticized Bachelor Apparatus below. Frampton writes, "The works are unclassifiable in any conventional sense; they are 'other' in the deepest sense of the word and this 'strangeness' is a consequence of their opposition to the mainstream of Western art after the Renaissance."[17] Frampton's writings, which underpin many of the thoughts expressed here, point to the relationship between "delay in glass" and a potential "delay in architecture" that this essay attempts to establish.

These modes of delay resist the kind of classification that inevitably results from visual objectivity's fixed point of reference. Like Poppaea's veil, the façades of Koolhaas's library have a positive presence and, in distancing the viewer, a specific function: They are something inserted *between*. These façades not only transmit the shadowy presences of forms *within* but also acknowledge equally amorphous forms *without*, specifically clouds, whose generic shapes are etched on the Paris and Périphérique façades. In this respect, Koolhaas's façades, like those of the Maison de Verre, also have a certain affinity with the *Large Glass*, whose upper panel is visually dominated by the image of a cloud. The cloud is an appropriate symbol of the new definition of transparency: translucent but dense, substantial but without definite form, eternally positioned between the viewer and the distant horizon. Koolhaas describes the library's façades as: "transparent, sometimes translucent, sometimes opaque; mysterious, revealing, or mute. Almost natural—like a cloudy sky at night, like an eclipse."[18]

The "mysterious" façades mentioned by Koolhaas and the "haze and evanescence" that Nouvel sees in the Cartier Foundation originate in conditions Rowe and Slutzky somewhat derisively refer to as the "haphazard superimpositions provided by the accidental reflections of light playing upon a translucent or polished surface."[19] But the architects' words are not simply poetic, and the effect they describe is not haphazard, as a brief excursion into quantum electrodynamics may suggest. Transparent and translucent materials allow some photons (particles of light) to pass through them while they partially reflect others. This activity in the surface of the transparent membrane can account for the reflection of as much as sixteen percent of the light particles that strike it, creating visible reflections and, frequently, a palpable luminescence.[20] The doubling of the glass found in many of the projects discussed here increases the potential for the glass surface to cast back photons: Up to ten percent of those that pass through the outer layer are reflected by the inner one; still others ricochet between the two. The dynamics of light passing through the transparent surfaces is described as a "slowing" of light by the physicist Richard Feynman.[21] The similarity of his term to Duchamp's "delay in glass" provides a striking bridge between the languages of the physicist and of the artist.

The contrast between one classic modernist project and these recent works illustrates the difference between today's attitudes toward the architectural surface and earlier conceptions of transparent and translucent skins. While capable of creating a remarkable complex surface, Mies van der Rohe intended to achieve the greatest transparency in his Tugendhat House (Brno, Czechoslovakia, 1929). To realize this aim, Mies employed the simplest kind of skin. The house was sheathed, floor to ceiling, by the largest sheets of transparent plate glass that had been produced in Europe at that time. Ironically, given its expense, he hoped that the glazing would be essentially a nonmaterial; in fact, a mechanism allowed the glass walls to be lowered into the basement, removing them altogether.

The projects discussed here rarely display a skin that can be called nonmaterial; instead, they exploit the positive physical characteristics of glass and other reflective substances. As opposed to the fraction of an inch by which the windows of the Tugendhat House separated its interior from the exterior, these newer projects frequently have very complex sections comprising a variety of materials, with discrete spaces in between.

This gives the surfaces a depth that is relatively slight—as in the tightly bound sheathing of the Signal Box 4 auf dem Wolf by Herzog and de Meuron (Basel, Switzerland, 1994)— and sometimes more pronounced, as in Peter Zumthor's Kunsthaus Bregenz (Bregenz, Austria, 1997), whose interior and exterior are separated by layers of translucent shingles, a passable air space, and an interior wall. Such built-up sections increase the emphasis on the architectural surface and reveal a desire for greater complexity, visual and otherwise, in the structure's skin. The reasons for multiple layers of material frequently include reducing the transmission of heat and cold, but the aim of insulating the structure is not solely a technical one. As does Poppaea's veil, layers of transparency define the viewer's relationship to the world, creating not only *insulation* but also a notable *isolation*—far removed from the continuum of space and experience implied by the nonmaterial surfaces of the Tugendhat House.

The tension between the viewer and object engendered by the use of veil-like, built-up membranes parallels a tension between architectural surface and architectural form that is evident in many of the works discussed here. The art historian Hubert Damisch has written at length about the invention of perspective drawing, one of the principal design tools used since the Renaissance, and its inherent bias towards form: "Perspective is able to comprehend only what its system can accommodate: things that occupy a place and have a shape that can be described by lines."[22] Damisch further notes that the limitations of perspective's ability to describe visual experience fully were apparent even at its inception. He cites Brunelleschi's 1417 experiment in which he tested the accuracy of his perspective drawing of the Baptistery of San Giovanni, seen from the door of the Cathedral in Florence. The drawing on a panel was held by the observer, who peered through a small hole in the back of it toward the Baptistery while holding at arm's length a mirror that reflected the right half of the panel, thus allowing him to compare the actual view of the structure with the reflection of Brunelleschi's drawing of it. Damisch notes that the architect attempted to compensate for the limitations he clearly saw in his drawing system: Having rendered the Baptistery and the surrounding square, Brunelleschi added a layer of silver leaf to the upper area of the panel to mirror the sky and the clouds, those aspects of the actual view that escaped his system of perspective. Brunelleschi's addition of silver leaf not only "manifests perspective as a structure of exclusion, the coherence of which is based upon a set of refusals," but, by reflecting the formlessness of the clouds, must "make room…for even those things which it excludes from its system."[23]

Many of the projects presented here exhibit a similarly compensatory attitude, an attempt to "make room" for that which neither perspective nor Cartesian space can describe. Dan Graham, in *Two-Way Mirror Cylinder inside Cube*, a component of his Rooftop Urban Park Project at the Dia Center for the Arts (New York City, 1991), recognizes the usefulness of geometry, plan organization, and systemization of the structure while refusing to assign them a transcendent, defining role. The environment, endlessly reflected, literally superimposes formlessness on the structure's architectural surfaces, easily overcoming the certitude of the structurally framed view and the idealized abstraction of the circle and the square that create its plan, dissolving their Platonic forms in contingent perceptions. Similarly, the transparent surfaces, flickering video screens, and tilted volume of the Glass Video Gallery by Bernard Tschumi (Groningen, the Netherlands, 1990) counteract the ability of a structural grid and perspective vision to determine the overall image of architecture. As Tschumi explains, "The appearance of permanence (buildings are solid; they are made of steel, concrete, bricks, etc.) is increasingly challenged by the immaterial representation of abstract systems (television and electronic images)."[24]

Rosalind Krauss has recently described a phenomenological reading of minimalist sculpture on the part of certain architecture critics that effects a shift in meaning that closely parallels the shift from form to surface evident in the projects presented here. She writes, "Far from having what we would call the fixed and enduring centers of a kind of formulaic geometry, Minimalism produces the paradox of a centerless, because shifting, geometry....Because of this demonstrable attack on the idea that works achieve their meaning by becoming manifestations or expressions of a hidden center, Minimalism was read as lodging meaning in the surface of the object, hence its interest in reflective materials, in exploiting the play of natural light."[25] This interpretation of minimalist sculpture's tendency to shift the meaning of the object from its form to its surface has broad implications for architecture. Jean Nouvel expresses a similar idea when he describes the architecture of his Cartier Foundation as one whose rules consist in "rendering superfluous the reading of solid volumes in a poetry of haze and evanescence."[26]

In telling contrast to the ultimate importance given to architectural form in both historicist postmodernism and deconstructivism, many of these projects exhibit a remarkable lack of concern for, if not antipathy toward, formal considerations. In fact, most of the projects could be described by a phrase no more complicated than "rectangular volume." Commenting on one of his recent projects, Koolhaas explains the logic of this formal restraint: "It is not a building that defines a clear architectural identity; but a building that creates and triggers potential."[27] The tension between surface and form in contemporary architecture is not limited to relatively simple forms: The overall silhouettes of Renzo Piano's Kansai International Airport (Osaka, 1994) or Nicholas Grimshaw and Partners' Waterloo International Terminal (London, 1994), for example, are far too complex to be characterized as minimalist. Kansai Airport's sheer scale prevents us from grasping its form, and the extent of the new Waterloo terminal can only be seen from the air. Yet even when experiencing parts of Kansai Airport, we realize that its silvery, undulating skin is more critical to its design than is its formal composition; equally, the form of the Waterloo International Terminal reflects peculiarities of the lot lines of existing rail yards rather than any preconceived formal conceit. In both projects, the overall form is complex but indefinable, specific but nonrepresentational.

None of the above structures, or any of the less articulated ones previously considered, displays interest in "timeless, unchanging geometries," and all of them complement the diminished importance of overall form by an increased sensitivity to the skin. And while the large projects may seem not just indifferent to but fundamentally estranged from the geometric rigors of perspectival construction, what impresses the viewer of a project such as Toyo Ito's Shimosuwa Municipal Museum (Shimosuwa, Japan, 1993) is not that its form is difficult to grasp—which it is—but that it simultaneously appears so precise.

In effect, it suggests a new conception of measure and order. Brunelleschi perceived an unbridgeable gap between the measurable (the Baptistery) and the immeasurable (such as a cloud). Similarly, Leonardo identified, as Damisch points out, two kinds of visible bodies, "of which the first is without shape or any distinct or definite extremities…. The second kind of visible bodies is that of which the surface defines and distinguishes the shape."[28] Leonardo's distinction is essentially false, however, determined by the inability of Renaissance mathematics to describe complex surfaces. Fractal geometry has shown that there is no such fundamental distinction between the Baptistery and the cloud, only a difference in the manner of calculating their physical characteristics.

The computer has diminished the realm of the immeasurable in architectural design. In describing the uniquely shaped panels that compose the skin of the Shimosuwa Museum, Ito noted that without computer technology, their cost—relative to that of standardized panels—would have been prohibitive. The use of extensive computer modeling in the design of Kansai Airport and Waterloo Terminal further demonstrates the extent to which technology has overcome the "problem" of structure, once a primary focus of design, whose "solution" subsequently defined, visually and otherwise, all other aspects of a project. This "relativization" of structure can be seen in various ways in the projects discussed in this essay; for example, Nagisa Kidosaki, writing about the Shimosuwa Museum, explains: "Thin membranes meant a thin structural system."[29]

The use of sophisticated computer modeling is only one sign of the impact of technology on the architectural surface. The incorporation of the electronic media into contemporary structures may result in the transformation of a building's skin, which literally became a screen for projection in Koolhaas's iconic unbuilt project for the Karlsruhe Zentrum fur Kunst and Medientechnologie (1989). A less spectacular but perhaps more architectonic synthesis of the electronic media can be seen in those projects in which electronic technology is not simply grafted to the structure but transformed into material and spatial qualities. The flattening of objects and activities projected onto translucent glazing gives a façade or interior surface the aura of a flickering electronic screen. On a small scale, this phenomenon is evident in the Thanhauser and Esterson gymnasium, where the athletes' silhouettes are projected onto the surfaces of dressing room cubicles (each cubicle has splayed walls, as if to suggest projection). On a larger scale, the farmhouses and elements of the natural landscape outside Ito's ITM Building collapse, in effect, as they are projected onto the surface glazing of the triple-height atrium. In Tod Williams and Billie Tsien's portable translucent set for the play *The World Upside Down* (Amsterdam and New York, 1990-91), projections actually became part of the performance as actors' silhouettes were cast onto screens and magnified by manipulation of the lighting. Jacques Herzog writes of "these surfaces for projection, these levels of overlapping, the almost-identity of architecture."[30]

Despite the ambiguous, equivocal, and at times even erotic undertones of many of the projects discussed here, it would be incorrect to assign them to a world of smoke and mirrors, where all is illusion, indecipherable and unattainable. Rather, they realign or rethink a nexus of ideas that has fueled much of architectural development since the Renaissance: perspectival vision, Cartesian space, and, by inference, the structural grid. Inherent in the works discussed in this essay is the possibility of a position that includes the certitude of objective vision and the equivocal nature of the gaze; these works recognize the efficacy and the utility of perspectival construction without subordinating all else to its language of measure and order. The fusion of the two might be best understood in the designers' attitude toward structure, for centuries the most evident expression of the theoretical coincidence of perspectival vision and Cartesian thinking. Many of these projects share a common approach to the relationship between the structure and the skin: The structural members, rather than framing and therefore defining the point of view, are lapped over by single and double layers of translucent sheathing, as in the interior partitions of the Cartier Foundation or the clerestory of the Goetz Collection. The structure, while providing support in a straightforward manner, has a diminished potential to determine the appearance of the building. Other projects here virtually erase the boundary between support and surface: the Glass Video Gallery makes no material distinction between the glass ribs that give it stability and the glass sheathing that encloses the space. The monocoque design of the unbuilt Phoenix Art Museum Sculpture Pavilion (1996) by Williams and Tsien similarly merges structure and sheathing. The Pavilion's translucent resin panels, ranging from one-half to one inch thick and connected only with stainless steel clips, are self-supporting and stabilizing.

It could be argued that these self-effacing but critical details "relativize" the role of the structure in a more self-confident way than deconstructivist ploys, such as tilted columns, destabilized surfaces, and structural redundancies. Meant to undermine the role of structure relative to architecture, these strategies frequently achieve the opposite. In contrast, the newer strategies considered here demonstrate that architectonic detailing can be unambiguous about creating ambiguity. Italo Calvino expresses this idea well: "Lightness for me goes with precision and determination, not vagueness and the haphazard."[31] In "Lightness," one of Calvino's *Six Memos for the Next Millennium*, he writes, "I look to science to nourish my visions in which all heaviness disappears"; and further, "The iron machines still exist, but they obey the orders of weightless bits."[32] Calvino reminds us that just as the current conception of transparency is distant from that held by early modern rationalists, these contemporary expressions of lightness are distinct from earlier conceptions of lightweight architecture: They imply a seeming weightlessness rather than a calculation of relative weight.[33] Calvino's balance between iron machines and weightless bits is also seen in Starobinski's prescription for the "reflexive gaze," which incorporates the wisdom associated with vision, yet "trusts in the senses and in the world the senses reveal."[34]

The subject of Starobinski and Calvino is literature, but their observations have numerous implications for understanding the aesthetics of the architecture discussed here, as well as its broader cultural context.[35] Calvino refers to Guido Cavalcanti as a poet of "lightness," which he defines as follows: "(1) it is to the highest degree light; (2) it is in motion; (3) it is a vector of information."[36] Ito's architectural installation in Yokohama, named the Tower of the Winds (1986–95), practically begs to be analyzed in these terms. Rising above a major traffic intersection, the structure was relatively nondescript in daylight but brought to life at night by thousands of computer-controlled light sources, whose constantly changing patterns responded to sounds and wind. In the architect's words, "The intention was to extract the flow of air (wind) and noise (sound) from the general flow of things in the environment of the project and to transform them into light signals, that is, visual information. Simply put, it was an attempt to convert the environment into information."[37]

It is not surprising that the pervasive presence in contemporary culture of film, television, video, and computer screens, representing a newfound sensibility of light, movement, and information, should find its way into architecture. Koolhaas's Karlsruhe Zentrum fur Kunst and Medientechnologie project is perhaps the most provocative configuration of the electronic screen and the architectural façade. Among built projects, Ito's Tower of the Winds, Tschumi's Glass Video Gallery, and Mehrdad Yazdani's CineMania Theatre (Los Angeles, 1994) represent more restrained uses of electronic imagery but still demonstrate the ability of the architectural object to be transformed by the dull glow and flickering image of the electronic media. The effect, as Ito has described it, is to render urban space as a "phenomenal city of lights, sounds, and images ... superimposed on the tangible urban space of buildings and civil engineering works."[38]

Ito is not alone in seeking architecture that "is to the highest degree light." *Floor Plan*, an installation by Melissa Gould (Linz, Austria, 1991), consisted of a nearly full-scale outline of the plan of a Berlin synagogue destroyed during the Nazi terror. The ghost building was evoked by lights in shallow trenches, which traced the configuration of the synagogue's walls and columns. Photographs document the poignant dramatic character of the project: we see eerily lit faces of visitors moving through the installation. More tragically, the work can disappear at the flick of a switch. Gould's project demonstrates unequivocally that "lightness" should not be confused with frivolity.

The current fascination with the architecture of lightness in many ways depends on recent technological developments. It also manifests a persistent theme in Western culture. Describing his proposed ABN-AMRO Head Office Building (Amsterdam, 1992), Harry Wolf refers to the "longstanding concern for light in the Netherlands; that is, the association of luminosity, precision, and probity in all matters." Notwithstanding the philosophical associations of light with the Enlightenment, illumination, and so on, however, the attempt to magnify the presence of natural light in northern European projects is primarily a response to the immediate setting—also a longstanding concern. Wolf recalls "Vermeer's preoccupation with subtle modulations of light through a window."[39] Jan Vermeer's emphasis on ambient light is, among other things, an attempt to magnify its diminished presence in northern latitudes; a similar motive led to the gilding of architectural features, from the cupolas of New Haven's churches and the Goldene Dachel of Munich's imperial residence to the reflective sheathing of Gehry's Weisman Art Museum (Minneapolis, 1993). This sensitivity to low levels of natural light also may be a response to the flattening of the shadowless landscape, particularly during the winter months.

Herzog usefully observes: "Le Corbusier...wrote, 'Architecture is the scientific, correct, and wonderful game of volumes assembled under light.' What, however, if architecture is not a game at all, especially not a scientific and correct one and if the light is often clouded over, diffuse, not so radiant as it is in the ideal southern landscape?"[40] Holl's Museum of Contemporary Art (Helsinki, 1993) traps this diffuse northern light within its section in order to introduce it, both directly and by reflection, into the lower parts of the building—

suggesting, perhaps, an architectural antithesis of Le Corbusier's *brise-soleil*, a shield from Mediterranean sunlight. Oriented to maximize exposure to the sun, which is low on the horizon most of the year, the museum incorporates a reflecting pool as an extension of nearby Toolo Bay. In Holl's words, "The horizontal light of northern lati- tudes is enhanced by a waterscape that would serve as an urban mirror, thereby linking the new museum to Helsinki's Toolo heart, which on a clear day, in [Alvar] Aalto's words, 'extends to Lapland.'"[41]

In climates far removed from the idealized, sun-filled landscape of the Mediterranean, which Le Corbusier encountered in his youthful *voyage en Orient*, the longing for light may conflict with another more recent cultural concern. The past two decades have seen an increasing consciousness of architecture's environmental implications, particularly the energy consumption of buildings. Two approaches, both of which avoid or minimize mechanical heating and cooling systems dependent on fuel consumption, attempt to balance environmental concerns with the widespread use of glass and other thermally inefficient materials.

The first approach is essentially passive, in the technical sense of employing non- mechanical systems to heat and cool structures and often electing to forgo optimal climate control. Williams and Tsien's Phoenix Art Museum Sculpture Pavilion was designed to have no mechanical air-conditioning system; instead, it would employ a low-technology cooling device based on commonsense thermodynamics. Approximately twenty feet above the viewing area, scores of nozzles would emit a fine mist of cool water, which would evaporate before reaching ground level. The heat exchange that occurs during the evaporation process would lower the air temperature by ten to twenty degrees, and this heavier air would then descends to cool visitors in the open pavilion. The Leisure Studio (Espoo, Finland, 1992) is an equally simple structure consisting of a thin layer of translucent polycarbonate sheathing over a wood frame. Designed by four young architects, Kaako, Laine, Liimatainen and Tirkkonen, as a sort of communal weekend retreat, the Leisure Studio employs no systems requiring high energy con- sumption to compensate for low thermal efficiency. Rather, users must simply accept constraints imposed by the climate: diminished comfort or restricted use when tempera- tures reach seasonal extremes. This attitude should not be perceived as a kind of obliviousness to the reality of climatic conditions but as a value judgment: a conscious decision reflecting a deep-rooted preference for the enhancement of available light, for one particular kind of comfort instead of another.

The second approach uses higher technology to achieve energy efficiency. Just as the computer has rendered the problem of structure less fundamental, limitations on the efficiency of mechanical heating and cooling are being overcome by technological advancements. Norman Foster's Business Promotion Center (Duisburg, Germany, 1993) is a building with an insulated glass façade wrapped in another layer of glass. A continu- ous air space between the two layers rises from the ground to the top of the structure. Large buildings, in contrast to smaller ones such as the Goetz Collection, absorb too much heat. To control heat intake, the air space in the Duisburg project has translucent louvers that can admit light but deflect heat, which can then be exhausted upward before entering the interior glazing. Within this system, there is an attempt to address micro environmental differences between interior spaces. Even though the louvers adjust themselves automatically to the position of the sun, office workers can readjust them. Occupants may also open windows in the inner glazing to ventilate offices from the air moving through the twenty-centimeter gap between the inner and outer glazing.

Just as lightness offers a way to understand much of contemporary architecture in terms other than formal ones, cultural concerns with light and the environment are not limited to glass structures. The shimmering skin of metal tiles that covers Kansai Airport not only evokes the architect's stated goal of "lightness," but also acts as a huge umbrella, protecting the structure from heat gain as well as rain. The building's undulating wave shape is, borrowing Calvino's words, "to the highest degree light," but it also interestingly embodies his emphasis on movement. Its shape expresses the flow of passengers across the structure from the "landside" to the "airside," as they move from check-in to departure, and it is also calculated to channel streams of air. The voluptuous interior ceiling carries ribbonlike channels, their shape derived from computer models of the flow of air, which guide heated and cooled air through the length of the building without the use of enclosed air ducts.

Such applications of innovative solutions to environmental problems bespeak a confidence in technology that has become discredited in some quarters. But the dismissal of a technological approach as evidence of an unjustified faith in the myth of progress is refuted by the successes of Foster, Piano, Peter Rice, and many other architects and engineers. Much of their research seeks to justify the ongoing use of glazed structures, so it is not surprising that their attention often focuses on glazing materials. While this research, like that devoted to conversion of solar energy, has limited application today, new glazing materials are on the edge of wide use. "Superwindows" with various coatings and gas-filled cavities have already proven to have better insulation properties than today's thermally efficient opaque materials.

Perhaps more intriguing than this new class of high-performance but essentially static systems are what Stephen Selkowitz and Stephen LaSourd call "smart" glazings, which react to changing conditions. These include "photochromic glass, which reversibly changes optical density when exposed to light," and "thermochromic glazings, which become translucent when a preset thermal threshold is reached."[42] The former, used in sunglasses, is not yet sold for architectural use, but the latter, according to the authors, will become more widely available in the near future. A third type of smart glazings, called electrochromic, consists of multilayer assemblies, through which a low-voltage electric current can be passed, causing ions to move to the outer layer where they may reflect heat-producing ultraviolet light but transmit visible wavelengths.

To speak of the technological attitudes of the projects discussed here as cultural phenomena requires further scrutiny, particularly given the prominence of glass structures over the course of this century. Glass architecture is not, however, unique to our time; a centuries-long fascination with it is evident in Jewish, Arabic, and European literature and mythology. As the architectural historian Rosemarie Haag Bletter has demonstrated, the "glass dream" that inspired these cultures has ancient roots, traceable to the biblical accounts of King Solomon's temple having reflective floors made of gold.[43] The glass dream was sustained through the Mozarabic culture of Medieval Spain, principally in literary form, but it also found built expression in small metaphorical structures such as garden pavilions. "Because an actual glass or crystal palace was not technically feasible, the semblance of such a building was attained through allusion: water and light were used to suggest a dissolution of solid materials into a fleeting vision of disembodied, mobile architecture."[44] In the Gothic period, the glass dream found greater expression in built form, in soaring cathedrals with their expansive walls of colored glass, as well as in literary sources, particularly the legends of the Holy Grail. In Wolfram von Eschenbach's *Parzifal*, the sought-after Holy Grail is symbolized by a glowing crystal hidden in a cave. The association between the image of a crystal or jewel and glass architecture is enduring. Zaha Hadid, describing her 1994 design for the Cardiff Bay Opera House, refers to the overall organization as an "inverted necklace" that strings together the various service elements, which she calls the "jewels" of the program.[45] Similarly, Harry Wolf speaks of his attempts to "create a heightened sense of transparency, just as light reflected and refracted in a gem seems more compelling and brilliant."[46]

This literary and architectural motive continued through the Renaissance, emerging as a central theme of Francesco Colonna's widely read *Hypnerotomachia Poliphili* of 1499. An expression of the romantic aspect of the Renaissance fascination with the ruins of classical antiquity, it invokes images of structures with transparent alabaster walls and floors of highly polished obsidian, so mirrorlike that viewers thought they were walking through the reflected sky. While the Enlightenment was characterized by a fascination with light and the scientific investigation of optics, its architectural expressions were not as poetic. The Crystal Palace might seem equally rationalist, though it is hard for us to imagine the impact of this first extensively glazed large structure, envisioned as the stage for a global event, and the spectacle created by its construction and dismantling. Furthermore, the glass fountain at its crossing was an understated but direct reference to the fantastic Mozarabic structures described by Bletter.[47]

As Bletter has demonstrated, the association of crystalline architecture with the transcendent (and its counterpart, the association of opaque materials with the profane) is central to the glass dream in all its manifestations. The expressionist movement in the twentieth century added to the spirituality, fantasy, transformation, and utopianism with which glass architecture had historically been identified. In the aftermath of the First World War, expressionists such as architect Bruno Taut were seeking not only new forms but also a new society. Bletter notes, "The crystalline glass house...concretizes for Taut the kind of unstructured society he envisions. Glass is here no longer the carrier of spiritual or personal transformation but of a political metamorphosis."[48]

In an essay published in 1984, K. Michael Hays proposes the possibility of a "critical architecture" that is perceived as a cultural phenomenon, as a readable text, without forgetting that it is a particular kind of text with specific references to its own history, "a critical architecture that claims for itself a place between the efficient representation of preexisting cultural values and the wholly detached autonomy of an abstract formal system."[49] If the architecture presented here can claim to occupy such a position, one might ask: Where is that place? Of what exactly is this contemporary architecture critical?

First and foremost, it is a critique of the canonical history of modern architecture. The historian Reyner Banham writes: "The official history of the Modern Movement, as laid out in the Twenties and codified in the Thirties, is a view through the marrow-hole of a dry bone .... The choice of a skeletal history of the movement with all the Futurists, Romantics, Expressionists, Elementarists and pure aesthetes omitted, though it is most fully expressed in [Siegfried] Giedion's Bauen in Frankreich, is not to be laid to Gideon's charge, for it was the choice of the movement as a whole. Quite suddenly modern architects decided to cut off half their grandparents without a farthing."[50]

The modern past is reconfigured by many of the projects discussed here in that they offer a chance to reconsider the reputations of certain figures whose work was largely ignored in the postwar period. Fritz Neumeyer uses terms strikingly similar to Starobinski's when describing Otto Wagner's Postal Savings Bank (Vienna, 1904–6): "Like the then floating garment that clothes the female body in ancient Greek sculpture, revealing as much beauty as it conceals, Wagner's treatment of the sculpture and construction exploits a similar kind of delicate, sensuous play that was probably only evident to a connoisseur of a certain age and experience. Exactly this principle gives the interior of the [Postal Savings Bank] its quality of silk-like transparency. The glass veil is lifted up on iron stilts that carefully cut into its skin and gently disappear."[51]

Paul Nelson's "technosurrealist"[52] Suspended House, a design for a glazed volume with free-floating forms suspended within, provides a model for Sejima's Women's Dormitory and a number of other projects presented here. Describing his unbuilt project of 1935, Nelson said, "Suspension in space...heightens the sense of isolation from the outside world."[53]

The Maison de Verre by Pierre Chareau, largely ignored by modern historians until the publication of Kenneth Frampton's monograph on Chareau in 1969, looms large in any discussion of lightness.[54] Recognized in its time as having transcended the then ossifying parameters of the International Style, it was referred to, by Nelson, as having a "cinematographic sense of space," a description that invokes much of the imagery employed here to describe contemporary architectural synergy.[55] In its visual complexity, the coyness with which it reveals its interior space, and its willful subordination of structural clarity, the façade of the Maison de Verre could serve as a précis for Starobinski's notion of the gaze as a reflexive act. Vidler's description of façades that reveal "shadowy presences" could equally be applied to Chareau's masterwork or Frank Lloyd Wright's Johnson Research Laboratory Tower (Racine, Wisconsin, 1944).

Oscar Nitzchke's seminal project of 1935, La Maison de la Publicité, was long neglected by modern historians, whose interests were more focused on the machine metaphor than on populist expressions of modern culture such as cinema and advertising.[56] Yet the project offers an early example of the current fascination with electronic media and the nocturnal transformation of architecture. Recalling Calvino's triad of light, movement, and information, Nitzchke's project assumes a prophetic aura. In postmodernism's caricature (ironically based largely on Giedion) of modern history, the wholesale devaluation of buildings such as Gordon Bunshaft's Beinecke Rare Book and Manuscript Library at Yale University (New Haven, CT, 1963) has further obscured the roots of a number of works discussed in this essay. The Beinecke's section within a section—an outer layer of translucent alabaster enclosing a glazed, climate-controlled rare books library—is revived in various ways in Peter Zumthor's Kunsthaus Bregenz and other projects included here.

In addition to representing an attempt to recapture lost figures in modern architectural history, these projects also reflect the current re-evaluation of the canonical masters. As a result of the historical parody of "glass boxes" offered by postmodern critics, a new generation is rediscovering an architecture of the not so recent past. Charles Jencks's dismissal of the work of Mies van der Rohe exemplifies postmodernist criticism: "For the general aspect of an architecture created around one (or a few) simplified values, I will use the term univalence. No doubt in terms of expression the architecture of Mies van der Rohe and his followers is the most univalent formal system we have, because it makes use of few materials and a single, right-angled geometry."[57] Detlef Mertins's writings are among recent, less hostile appraisals: "Could it be that this seemingly familiar architecture is still in many ways unknown, and that the monolithic Miesian edifice refracts the light of interpretation, multiplying its potential implications for contemporary architectural practices?"[58] Mertins could well be speaking of the Leisure Studio or Koolhaas's Two Patio Villas (Rotterdam, 1988), in which the use of clear, frosted, green-tinted, and armored glass recalls not the nonmaterial of the Tugendhat House but the rich surfaces and the multiplicity of perceptions evident in Mies's Barcelona Pavilion.

Although the expressionists were rejected by rationalist architects such as Hilberseimer and effectively written out of the history of modern architecture by Giedion and others, the influence of Taut and his followers, referred to as the Glass Chain, is evident on the work of a number of canonical modern masters, including Mies's glass skyscrapers of about 1920. Walter Gropius, in his manifesto for the Bauhaus, was influenced by Taut's expressionist utopianism: "Together let us desire, conceive, and create the new structure of the future, which will embrace architecture and sculpture and painting in one unity and will one day rise toward heaven from the hands of a million workers like the crystal symbol of a new faith."[59] Frampton, Banham, and others have noted that standard modern histories frequently underestimate the important relationships between what have come to be perceived as irreconcilably opposed tendencies.

The success of Rowe and Slutzky in awakening a generation of American—and to a lesser extent, European—architects from the "glass dream" over the course of four decades depended on establishing a more narrow dialectic than the fundamental one between transparency and opacity described by Bletter. Given Rowe's nostalgia for the classical façade and his antipathy toward technological imagery, that longstanding relationship was enormously inconvenient. Rowe and Slutzky inverted the dichotomy by equating the literal transparency of glass structures with materiality and the phenomenal transparency of Le Corbusier with the higher functions of intellectual abstraction: "A basic distinction must perhaps be established. Transparency may be an inherent quality of substance—as in a wire mesh or glass curtain wall, or it may be an inherent quality of organization…a phenomenal or seeming transparency."[60]

If much of the architecture discussed here can be seen as a critical response to Giedion and the "room of shadowless light" that he helped canonize, it also represents a critique of the formalism espoused by Rowe in the course of devaluing glass architecture. The façades seen here express not only a post-Rovian sense of transparency, but also the rejection of the frontally viewed classical façade and its "structure of exclusion," its "set of refusals." While there is a common interest in maintaining a high level of ambiguity, in limiting the overreaching certitude of architectural expression, this recent architecture goes beyond evoking the "equivocal emotions" that Rowe and Slutzky found in the presence of architectural form, investigating the possibility of rethinking—and investing with meaning—the architectural skin. As membranes, screens, and filters, the surfaces of this architecture establish a vertigo of delay, blockage, and slowness, upending the "vertigo of acceleration" that has dominated architectural design since the invention of perspectival drawing.

In a contemporary context, the critique of Rowe's Epicureanism represented by the projects discussed here need not be taken as endorsement of a new *sachlich* architecture of shadowless light, an expression of a renewed Puritanism of our time. Just the opposite: This recent architecture, trusting in "the senses and in the world the senses reveal," can be described as beautiful—a word heard infrequently in architectural debates. Indeed, academic rationalists enjoyed such success in establishing the basis for architectural discussions that architects have been called "secret agents for beauty." As a group, the projects included in this essay have a compelling visual attraction, undiminished by close reflection, that implicitly criticizes Hilberseimer's rejection of the aesthetic dimension. They likewise reject the strictures of postmodernism, which have alternated between invoking, as inspirations for architecture, a suffocating supremacy of historical form and arid philosophical speculation. Of the latter Koolhaas writes, "Our amalgamated wisdom can be caricatured: according to Derrida we cannot be Whole, according to Baudrillard we cannot be Real, according to Virilio we cannot be There—inconvenient repertoire for a profession helplessly about being Whole, Real, and There."[61]

In Tony Kushner's 1994 play *Angels in America, Part Two: Perestroika* opens with Aleksii Antedilluvianovich Prelapsarianov, the World's Oldest Living Bolshevik, haranguing the audience: "What System of Thought have these Reformers to present to this mad swirling planetary disorganization, to the Inevident Welter of fact, event, phenomenon, calamity?"[62] Prelapsarianov's taunts reminded us that the already muddied waters of the postmodern debate, played out over the last thirty years, we are being even further roiled by millennial fervor, with its own set of critical and emotional references. Even so, without claiming an overreaching system of thought, it is possible to see in the current architectural synergy further evidence of what Vidler referred to as a renewed adherence to the spirit of the age, a spirit that most often expressed itself as one of invention and idealism. In response to the "inconvenient repertoire" of poststructuralism, Koolhaas imagines a "potential to reconstruct the Whole, resurrect the Real, reinvent the collective, reclaim maximum possibility."[63]

Beyond his own work, Koolhaas's words resonate in projects at vastly different scales, although, as is often the case, they can be most distinctly seen in smaller projects, where simpler programs allow for more direct expression. Despite its modest scale, the Leisure Studio eloquently fits Hays's definition of a critical architecture, but it is also an expression of an idealism too easily dismissed in a cynical age. Designed by an architectural collaborative as a *contre-projet* in response to an official housing exhibition, it has subsequently been used as an informal meeting place where artists and architects socialize and exchange ideas. In contrast to standard professional practice, the structure was built and paid for by the architects themselves. Tod Williams and Billie Tsien's mobile, translucent stage set evokes the choreographer's theme of societal transformation, and in doing so reminds us that the realm of the aesthetic has social dimensions. Graham's *Two Way Mirror Cylinder inside Cube*, a work that clearly occupies a position "in between," consciously refers to the history of glass architecture. But Graham's work, too, transcends a purely aesthetic approach. By incorporating it into his Rooftop Urban Park Project, which he characterizes as a "utopian presence" in the city, he elevates the work from the status of mere formal abstraction. His contemporary urban park—which, like its traditional counterparts, seeks to reintegrate alienated city dwellers with their environment while providing a contemplative place apart—restores the aesthetic dimension of the glass dream and points toward the idealism that sustained it.

1. Ludwig Hilberseimer, "Glasarchitektur," *Die Form* 4 (1929): 522. Translated by Vera Neukirchen.

2. Ibid., 521.

3. Jean Starobinski, "Poppaea's Veil," in *The Living Eye* (Cambridge: Harvard University Press, 1989), 1.

4. Michel de Montaigne, *The Essays of Michel de Montaigne*, trans. And ed. M.A Screech (London: Allen Lane, Penguin Press, 1991), 697. The passage continues: "Why do women now cover up those beauties—right down below their heels—which every woman wants to display and every man wants to see? Why do they clothe with so many obstacles, layer upon layer, those parts which are the principal seat of our desires—and of theirs? And what use are those defense-works with which our women have started to arm their thighs, if not to entrap our desired and to attract us by keeping us at a distance?"

5. Starobinski, "Poppaea's Veil," 1-2.

6. Ibid., 2.

7. See note 4.

8. Yoshiharu Tsukamoto, "Toyo Ito: An Opaque 'Transparency,'" in JA Library 2, special issue of *The Japan Architect* (Summer 1993): 154.

9. Colin Rowe and Robert Slutzky, "Transparency: Literal and Phenomenal," in Rowe, *The Mathematics of the Ideal Villa and Other Essays* (Cambridge: MIT Press, 1992), 221.

10. Anthony Vidler, *The Architectural Uncanny: Essays in the Modern Unhomely* (Cambridge: MIT Press, 1992), 221.

11. Rowe and Slutzky, "Transparency," 163-164.

12. In a recent communication with the author, the architectural historian Joan Ockman summarized the elements of phenomenal transparency as "free play in the object, the extension of 'aesthetic time,' and oscillating readings or meanings that are ultimately unresolvable." Her description clearly shows that a foundation of Gestalt psychology, provided by her husband Robert Slutzky, supported the concept of phenomenal transparency.

13. Rowe and Slutzky, "Transparency," 171.

14. Kenneth Frampton, "Pierre Chareau, and Eclectic Architect," in Marc Vellay and Frampton, *Pierre Chareau, Architect and Craftsman, 1883–1950* (New York: Rizzoli, 1985), 243.

15. Octavio Paz, *Marcel Duchamp, or The Castle of Purity*, trans. D. Gardner (London: Cape Goliard Press, 1970), 1-2. I am indebted to Peter Eisenman for suggesting that I look at Paz's discussion of transparency.

16. Frampton, "Pierre Chareau, an Eclectic Architect," 242.

17. Ibid.

18. Rem Koolhaas and Bruce Mau, S,M,L,XL (New York: Monacelli Press, 1995 [prepublication copy]), 654.

19. Rowe and Slutzky, "Transparency," 166.

20. Richard P. Feynman, *QED: The Strange Theory of Light and Matter* (Princeton: Princeton University Press, 1985), 69. I thank Guy Nordenson for suggesting Feynman's writings.

21. Ibid., 109.

22. Hubert Damisch, *Théorie du nuage* (Paris: Editions du Seuil, 1972), 170. Translated by Pierre Adler. I owe to Rosalind Krauss my introduction to Damisch's book, to which she refers in the essay cited in note 25.

23. Ibid.

24. Bernard Tschumi, "Groningen, Glass Video Gallery, 1990," in *Event-Cities* (Cambridge: MIT Press, 1994), 133-34.

25. Krauss, "Minimalism: The Grid, The/Cloud/, and the Detail," in Detlef Mertins, ed., *The Presence of Mies* (Princeton: Princeton Architectural Press, 1994), 133-34.

26. Jean Nouvel, "The Cartier Building," architect's statement, n.d.

27. Koolhaas and Mau, S,M,X,XL, 1261.

28. Leonardo da Vinci, *The Notebooks of Leonardo da Vinci*, arr., trans., and intro. E. MacCurdy (New York: George Braziller, 1939), 986-87.

29. Nagisa Kidosaki, "Shimosuwa Municipal Museum," in JA Library 2, special issue of *The Japan Architect* (Summer 1993): 27.

30. Jacques Herzog, architect's statement, n.d.

31. Italo Calvino, "Lightness," in *Six Memos for the Next Millennium* (New York: Vintage International, 1993), 16.

32. Ibid., 8.

33. The linguistic relationship between lightness and lightweight exists principally in English.

34. Starobinski, "Poppaea's Veil," 6.

35. For further analysis of Calvino and lightness in architecture, see Cynthia Davidson and John Rajchman, eds., *Any Magazine* 5 (March/April 1994).

36. Calvino, "Lightness," 13.

37. Toyo Ito, "A Garden of Microchips: The Architectural Image of the Microelectronic Age," in *JA Library* 2, special issue of *The Japan Architect* (Summer 1993): 11-13.

38. Ibid., 11.

39. Harry Wolf, "ABN-AMRO Head Office Building," architect's statement, n.d.

40. Jacques Herzog, "The Hidden Geometry of Nature," *Quaderns*, no. 181-82 (1989): 104.

41. Steven Holl, "Museum of Contemporary Art, Helsinki," architect's statement, n.d.

42. Stephen Selkowitz and Stephen LaSourd, "Amazing Glass," *Progressive Architecture* 6 (June 1994), 109.

43. Rosemarie Haag Bletter, "The Interpretation of the Glass Dream–Expressionist Architecture and the History of the Crystal Metaphor," *Journal of the Society of Architectural Historians* 40, no.1 (March 1981): 20.

44. Bletter, "Glass Dream," 25.

45. Zaha Hadid, "Cardiff Bay Opera House Architectural Competition," architect's statement, n.d.

46. Wolf, "ABN-AMRO Head Office Building."

47. Prince Albert Saxe-Coburg, the royal patron of the Crystal Palace, commissioned Edward Lorenzo Percy to design a centerpiece based on literary accounts of a fountain in the Alhambra. See Hermione Hobhouse, *Prince Albert: His Life and Work* (London: Hamish Hamilton Limited/The Observer, 1983), 103 (caption).

48. Bletter, "Glass Dream," 37.

49. Michael Hays, "Critical Architecture: Between Culture and Form," *Perspecta* (The Yale Architectural Journal) 21 (1984): 15.

50. Reyner Banham, "The Glass Paradise," *Architectural Review* 125, no. 745 (February 1959): 88.

51. Fritz Neumeyer, "Iron and Stone: The Architecture of Großstadt," in H.F. Mallgrave, ed., *Otto Wagner: Reflections on the Raiment of Modernity* (Santa Monica, Calif.: Getty Center for the History of Art and the Humanities, 1993), 134f.

52. Kenneth Frampton, "Paul Nelson and the School of Paris," in Joseph Abram and Terence Riley, eds., *The Filter of Reason: Work of Paul Nelson* (New York, Rizzoli, 1990), 12.

53. Judith Applegate, interview with Paul Nelson, *Perspecta* 13/14 (April 1971): 75-129.

54. Kenneth Frampton, "Maison de Verre," *Perspecta* (The Yale Architectural Journal) 12 (1968): 77-126. For further discussion of the relationship between Nelson and Chareau, see Abram and Riley, eds., *The Filter of Reason: Work of Paul Nelson* (New York, Rizzoli, 1990).

55. Paul Nelson, "La Maison de la Rue Saint-Guillaume," *L'architecture d'aujourd'hui 4me année*, ser. 3, vol. 9(Nov.–Dec. 1933): 9.

56. For an interesting but somewhat incomplete account of the relationship between Nitzchke, Nelson, and Chareau, see Sean Daly, "Composite Modernism: The Architectural Strategies of Paul Nelson and Oscar Nitzchke," *Basilisk* [journal online] 1, no.1 (1995), available at http://swerve.basilik.com.

57. Charles Jencks, *The Language of Post-Modern Architecture* (New York: Rizzoli, 1977), 15.

58. Detlef Mertins, "New Mies," in Mertins, ed., *The Presence of Mies* (New York: Princeton Architectural Press, 1994), 23.

59. Bletter, "Glass Dream," 38.

60. Rowe and Slutzky, "Transparency," 161.

61. Koolhaas and Mau, S,M,L,XL, 969.

62. Tony Kushner, *Angels in America: A Gay Fantasia on National Themes, Part II: Perestroika* (New York: Theater Communications Group, 1994), 13-14.

63. Koolhaas and Mau, S,M,L,XL, 510.

K/R–designed metal curtain,
Palm Island House (see page 78).

# John Keenen
# Terence Riley
## Nathan McRae

## K/R Staff, 1984-2007

John Beard
Aaron Bentley
Sofia Castricone
James Cleary
Jan Greben
Joe Serrins
David Small
Raul Smith
SiAe Sung
Jim Yohe
Robert Young
Patricia Bosch
Leslie Jill Hanson
Bruce Irwin
Seung Jae Lee
Cindy Rodriguez
David Paskin
Mile Verovic
Vanessa Ah-Chuen
Robert Aydlett

Sunil Bald
Neal Beckstedt
John Blackmon
Mark Cameron
Jeremy Carvalho
Steven Chang
Laurent Charlet
Natalie Cline
Mary Beth Comins
F. Greg Doench
Alfonso D'Onofrio
Godfrey Edwards
Jeremy Edminston
Makram El-Kadi
Alexander Eng
Anna Frens
Antonio Furgiuele
Richard Ingles
Susan Jennings
Engin Baris Kansu
Jamie Katz
Beth Ann Kelley
Eric Kerley
Daniel Kocieniewski
David Magid
Tina Manus
Stephen Martin
David McAlpine
Alan Metcalfe
Si Yeon Min
Garrick Montana
Brett Oberholzer
Toby O'Rorke
Carol Overby
Debra Pitkin
Michael Randazzo
Sabina Schlapfer
Phil Schmerbeck
Francesco Ceriani
Sebregondi
Joel Schifflet
John Shuttleworth
Myounghi Sul

Kees Stahl
Stanley Stinnett
Leah Strugess
John Truso
Celeste Umpierre
Max von Rudzinski
Jesse Walton
Patrick Walker
Mark Watkins
Dan Wood
Josh Adlin
Jamie Bush
Katerina Chatzikonstantinou
Francois Charbonnet
Jennifer Denlinger
Stephen Fox
Doh Lee
Yuki Kubota
Lukas Lenherr
Leonard Leung
John Maatman
Yves Macherel
Marcus Mangler
Lucy O'Sullivan
Lucien Tinga

ACKNOWLEDGMENTS

SPECIAL THANKS
Larry Allen
Emilio Ambasz
The Architectural League
   of New York
John Bennett
Clarissa Bronfman
Edgar Bronfman Jr.
Coco Brown
Andy Bush
Alice Chung
Carlos Cisneros
Gustavo Cisneros
Patricia Phelps de Cisneros
Pierre D'Arenberg
Bill Durgin
Ann ffolliott
Simone Fitz
Kenneth Frampton
Randy Fuchs
Cris Gabarron
Tony Goldman
Adriana Cisneros Griffin
Pat Hearn

Robert Herrmann
John Howard
Lauren Howard
Susan Henshaw Jones
Jenn Joy
Willi Kunz
Yvon Lambert
Leonard Lieberman
Nancy Lieberman
Jennifer McSweeney
Ambra Medda
Paul Morris
Omnivore
Jeff Preiss
Rebecca Quaytman
Lee Ramer
Lawrence Ramer
Craig Robins
Margit Rowell
Mayer Rus
Helen Searing
Julie Saul
Gary Schaevitz
Andrea Schwan
Scot Schy
Charlie Thompson
John Waddell
Linda Wells
Sid Wexler
Fehmi Zeko

MORE THANKS
Susan Ainsworth
Donald Albrecht
Cindy Allen
Sandra Antelo-Suarez
Sarah Auld
Pat Arnett
Raul Barreneche
Joan Bassin
Ed Baum
Barry Bergdoll
Kathryn Biddinger
Claudia Brandenberg
Muriel Brandolini
Nuno Brandolini
Sebastian Brandolini
Mary Bright
Dominique Browning
Don Bruning
Ellen Bruno
Bureau, NYC
Barry Canter
Amy Cappellazzo
Walter Chatham
Aric Chen
Craig Costello
Abraham Cuellar
Corey Delany
Deborah Dietsch
Livio Dimitriu
Scott Elliot
Michael Feldman

Martin Filler
Elaine Frank
Peter Galdi
Raymond Gastil
Tad Gawel
Robert Gober
The Graham Foundation
Fergus Grant
Steven Gretenstein
Mark Hage
Jonathan Hammer
Hello, NYC
Sarah Henry
David Holtzman
Mayda Andaya Horstmann
Reginald Hough
Iron, LA
Bruno Jakob
Anita Jorgensen
Brian Kish
Connie Koch
David Kufferman
Beth Lochtefeld
The MacDowell Colony
Sean MacPherson
Mike Maloney
Matthew Marks
Marlene McCarty
Donald Moffett
Seamus Moran
The Moran Foundation
Toshiko Mori
Herbert Muschamp
Gloria Naftali
New York Foundation
    for the Arts
Anne Nixon
Philip Nobel
Curbie Oestreich
Carol Overby
Nilay Oza
Proun Studio Space
Nicholas Quennell
Barry Richman
Mark Robbins
Manuel Rodriguez
Attila Rona
Margaret Russell
Joel Sanders
Jorge Silvetti
Jane Smith
Hiroko Sueyoshi
Saif Sumaida
Matt Streeter
Elizabeth Sverbeyeff Byron
Marek Teklinski
Thomas Thompson
Matthew Tirshwell
The Tony Smith Estate
Henry Urbach
Edwina von Gal
Pilar Vilades
Walid Wahab
Glenn Weiss
Wexner Center for the Arts
Peter Wheelwright

www.krnyc.com

## Photo and Drawing Credits

# K/R Project Index